WWE V. ~~~~~~~~~~ **ALL OUT**

VOL. 2

WRESTLETALK

Copyright Trident Digital Media Ltd. © 2023

All rights reserved.

No part of this book may be reproduced in any form or by any electronic or mechanical means, including information storage and retrieval systems, without written permission from the author, except for the use of brief quotations in a book review.

The views expressed in this book are solely those of the individual writers and do not reflect the opinions of WrestleTalk, Trident Digital Media Ltd., or any other affiliated companies.

CONTENTS

Foreword — Oli Davis … v

RULE OF ENGAGEMENT #11: Form strategic alliances to strengthen your position … xiii

1. SLIDING DOORS
   H G McLaren … 1

RULE OF ENGAGEMENT #12: Promote your best lieutenant when the time is right … 9

2. STILL GAME: TRIPLE H TO THE RESCUE?
   John Ellul … 11

RULE OF ENGAGEMENT #13: Do not tolerate any infighting among your troops … 29

3. BRAWL OUT
   H G McClaren … 31

RULE OF ENGAGEMENT #14: Change strategy if you're losing territory … 47

4. THE BIG PIVOT
   H G McLaren … 49

RULE OF ENGAGEMENT #15: Ensure your army has the deepest war chest … 65

5. THEY'VE NEVER HAD IT SO GOOD
   Dave Bradshaw … 67

RULE OF ENGAGEMENT #16: Know that a single moment can change the entire war … 81

6. THE WEEK THAT SHOOK THE WORLD
   Dave Bradshaw … 83

RULE OF ENGAGEMENT #17: Be prepared to mount a bloodless coup if necessary … 99

7. THE FINAL DAYS OF VINCE MCMAHON
   Dave Bradshaw … 101

RULE OF ENGAGEMENT #18: Open a new front in the war if circumstances warrant it … 115

8. COLLISION COURSE: CM PUNK, AEW, AND A COMPANY AT A CROSSROADS — 117
John Ellul

RULE OF ENGAGEMENT #19: Act swiftly at the first hint of mutiny — 133

9. STRAIGHT EDGE, HIGH STAKES: A LOOK BACK AT CM PUNK'S TIME IN AEW — 135
Connel Rumsey and Dee Adams

RULE OF ENGAGEMENT #20: Enlist those who know the enemy best — 149

10. COPING MECHANISM: WHY AEW NEEDS ADAM COPELAND TO BE A SUCCESS — 151
John Ellul

Afterword — 165
About the Authors — 167

FOREWORD
OLI DAVIS

Wrestling in the Summer of 2022 began with an exciting new dawn. Vince McMahon left WWE, publicly announcing on Twitter: "At 77, time for me to retire." Coincidentally at the same time there were mounting allegations against him of sexual misconduct and "hush money" payments.

He was gone. Really gone. For real. Probably. It would totally, definitely stick.

It lasted six months.

But for that summer optimism was rife. For the first time in forty years, there was a Vince McMahon-shaped void in the professional wrestling industry.

In his place stepped Paul Levesque, Triple H, the Cerebral Assassin, the King of Kings, the Game, Big Daddy Trips.

But this wasn't just a simple passing of the torch. This was a complete overhaul of WWE's creative direction. The atmosphere backstage transformed almost overnight. Superstars who had been lurking in the shadows of mid-card purgatory suddenly found new life. Storylines became more coherent, more gripping, and dare I say, more entertaining. The WWE Universe started to buzz with anticipation every week, eager to see what new twist or turn would come next. They would go on the most consistent run of quality pay-per-views in decades.

Nowhere was this more apparent than one of WWE's most captivating and masterfully crafted storylines in recent memory - the Bloodline saga. AEW had pushed great in-ring wrestling as its unique selling point. So smartly, Triple H focused on the sports entertainment. The captivating soap opera storyline stood out in the white noise of four-and-a-half star matches on free television every week (I'm not complaining, simply pointing out an effect of oversaturation).

This wasn't just another feud; it was a Shakespearean drama set in the squared circle, a tale of family, power, betrayal, and legacy, led by the Tribal Chief, Roman Reigns.

Reigns, along with his cousins, The Usos and Solo Sikoa, the eager-to-please Sami Zayn, and the wise counsel of Paul Heyman, transformed into a dominant, almost mythical force in WWE. Each week, they wove a complex tapestry of loyalty and power struggles, blurring the lines between reality and fiction, heroes and villains. The sheer charisma and intensity Reigns brought to the (head of the) table was mesmerising. He wasn't just a champion; he was the emperor of his own empire, ruling with an iron fist, and, most fascinatingly, a viciously insecure streak. I mean, who else demands acknowledgement in every city they walk into? It's almost like he's trying to convince himself.

FOREWORD

But what set the Bloodline storyline apart was its ability to keep the audience on the edge of their seats. Twists and turns were aplenty, with alliances tested and familial bonds strained. It was storytelling at its finest, reminiscent of the Attitude Era's best narratives, but with a modern twist that resonated with today's audience.

The impact of this storyline was profound. It reinvigorated interest in WWE, not just among the faithful but also among lapsed fans who had long turned their backs on the product, and newer viewers. Social media buzzed with discussions and theories, while ratings saw a much-needed boost. In an era where WWE's creative direction was often criticized, the Bloodline saga stood as a testament to what the company could achieve with compelling storytelling and strong character development.

This wasn't just good wrestling; it was good television. And as we'll see, it played a crucial role in the ongoing tussle for wrestling supremacy between WWE and AEW, a battle that, as this anthology will reveal, was full of surprises and dramatic twists.

Surprising and dramatic twists in AEW segway...

The Summer of 2022 over in Jacksonville had a looming storm approaching on the horizon. News of Triple H replacing Vince McMahon was already very concerning, with AEW now set to face a more coherent week-to-week competition. But it was the onscreen and backstage behaviour of CM Punk that would cause them the most issues.

When Punk made his AEW debut on an episode of Rampage in front of a raucous crowd in his home town of Chicago, it truly felt as though it could be enough to sway the pendulum in AEW's favour. It boosted TV ratings and brought a renewed sense of excitement and legitimacy to the promotion.

The self-proclaimed 'best in the world' seemed invigorated, excited to work with a new generation of talent. He quickly entered into a feud with Darby Allin, followed by a short but intense program with Eddie Kingston, and my favourite feud of modern times, against MJF.

It is no secret within the professional wrestling industry that CM Punk can be difficult to work with. He's passionate about the business and can often be outspoken as a result. Whilst fans were thrilled to have him in AEW, the same can not be said for all those backstage as tensions quickly began to rise. Reports of internal disagreements between Punk and The Elite began to circulate and rumours emerged that CM Punk had gotten his former best friend Colt Cabana blackballed from the company, rumours that Punk denied and attributed to The Elite.

Things came to a head at the All Out PPV on 4th September 2022. After winning the AEW Championship, Punk decided to do a modern day equivalent of his WWE pipebomb promo at the post-show media scrum. He criticised The Elite, referred to Adam Page as an "empty headed dumb f*ck," and invited anyone who has a problem with him to his locker room.

So The Elite confronted Punk backstage in what became known as 'Brawl Out', a reported six minute punch-up between The Elite, Punk, and Punk's trainer Ace Steel. It wasn't a good look for AEW or Tony Khan, who very much looked like he'd lost control of his own company. Instead of looking like a viable competitor to the WWE, AEW now looked exceptionally carny, unprofessional even. Both CM

FOREWORD

Punk and the Elite were removed from television and their titles were vacated.

The Elite would return weeks later at the Full Gear PPV, but it would be months and months before wrestling fans were to see Punk again - where he continued to cause issues, calling out Jon Moxley and Chris Jericho in a social media rant. In May 2023, however, AEW debuted its new weekly show, Collision, built entirely around CM Punk. It kind of felt like he was rewarded for bad behaviour by getting his own show.

The supposed strategy was to keep Punk on Collision and the Elite on Dynamite, a soft brand split solution that would never work in the long term. In theory, the backstage area would be a harmonious place, where everyone got along well and any disagreements could be discussed calmly and rationally. Absolutely no one would ever feel the need to express their displeasure using violence and...

'GLASS SHATTERS NOISE'

Nope, not Stone Cold. Enter 'Jungle Boy' Jack Perry.

The 27th August 2023 should have been a crowning achievement for AEW, putting on the record breaking All In pay-per-view from Wembley Stadium. But unfortunately, a lot of chatter was about the alleged brawl that happened between CM Punk and Jack Perry backstage at the event. Perry had gloated on-air about using real glass in a match, which was against Punk's wishes. Punk allegedly confronted Perry backstage. Another physical altercation took place, and Tony Khan decided to fire Punk the next day, losing his biggest star in the process.

The drama of losing, then regaining, then losing a highly controversial figure wasn't unique to AEW, though. Back in WWE, January 2023 saw a move that was shocking but also kind of not: Vince McMahon utilised his status as the company's largest shareholder, reshuffled the board and reappointed himself as executive chairman. He told media outlets that as the controlling shareholder, it was important for him to be involved in negotiations for the sale of the company, and he could support the management team best if he were the executive chairman. Credit where credit is due, he must've done a pretty stellar job supporting the management team because on 3rd April 2023, Vince McMahon stood side by side with UFC president, Dana White, and Endeavor CEO, Ari Emmanuel, to announce a super-merger, TKO, which was valued at a whopping $21 billion dollars. Endeavor would take a 51% share per cent in TKO, while WWE shareholders would control the remaining 49%. What's more, Vince was going to continue on at TKO as executive chairman. Despite the controversies of the past few years, it seemed Vince McMahon and the strange little caterpillar that had taken residence on his top lip (he had grown a moustache) were going to be able to sail off into the sunset after all. Or were they? By the end of the year, McMahon looked like he had been increasingly sidelined in his own company - and the legal controversies were far from settled either.

There was still another twist to come in Punk's story too. Just weeks before we went to press with this book, he made a jaw-dropping return to WWE at Survivor Series, marking one of the most astonishing comebacks in wrestling history. This wasn't just a surprise; it was a moment that redefined what the word 'unpredictable' means in the wrestling world. The crowd's reaction was electric, a mixture of shock, excitement, and sheer disbelief. Social media erupted, with fans and pundits alike trying to make sense of this seismic shift.

X

FOREWORD

CM Punk WWE return confirmed.

But what does this mean for WWE, AEW, and the wrestling industry as a whole? As we turn the page on this foreword and dive into the articles that comprise this anthology, we explore not just the events themselves, but their broader implications. We delve into the strategies, the behind-the-scenes machinations, and the personalities that have shaped this ongoing battle for wrestling supremacy. The following pages are more than just a collection of articles; they are a tapestry of stories, insights, and analyses that capture the essence of this incredible period in wrestling history.

So, whether you're a die-hard wrestling fan or a curious observer, there's something in these pages for you. This has been a truly ridiculous period in wrestling history, and I'm proud that our awesome team at WrestleTalk Magazine provided some of the best coverage available as it all took place.

So welcome to 'WWE vs. AEW - Fallout'. The story continues...

RULE OF ENGAGEMENT #11: FORM STRATEGIC ALLIANCES TO STRENGTHEN YOUR POSITION

By April 2022, AEW had already developed the beginnings of a relationship with New Japan Pro Wrestling (NJPW), with some limited talent sharing having taken place between the two promotions for over a year. Nonetheless, the industry was still set abuzz when company presidents Tony Khan and Takami Ohbari appeared on Dynamite to announce that they would be co-promoting a supershow. The event was to be called 'Forbidden Door', named after the portal that Khan claimed had been opened when the two companies started working together the previous year, and it would take place on 26th June at the United Center in Chicago. Coming soon after WWE enjoyed a triumphant WrestleMania 38 weekend, this felt like a major counteroffensive from Khan - an alliance with the biggest wrestling brand outside of North America.

Tickets sold out almost immediately when they became available in early May, and the pay-per-view broadcast attracted 125,000 buys - down slightly on AEW's most recent efforts, but respectable enough to suggest that the collaboration had legs. It was easy to see why those on the inside saw the deal as win-win: for both it was an opportunity to expand its global footprint and to present 'dream matches' that would be the stuff of fantasy for fans who followed both companies. That's not to say that planning such an event was easy: logistical hurdles, arguments over match placements, ensuring storyline continuity for both promotions and protecting talent on both sides all made for a tricky balancing act. But somehow it all came together and created a memorable night in the Windy City.

The event itself felt a bit surreal: watching Orange Cassidy wrestle Will Ospreay felt like watching two separate universes merge, as did seeing Jay White and Kazuchika Okada wrestling the likes of Adam Page and Adam Cole. Zack Sabre Jr's match against Claudio Castagnoli was special in another way, as the latter was a surprise replacement for the injured Bryan Danielson, and the latest example of how AEW had the ability to lure disillusioned talent away from Vince McMahon's empire. And then there was the main event: Jon Moxley, who had blazed the trail now being trodden by Castagnoli, versus New Japan icon Hiroshi Tanahashi. This match, in particular, was a litmus test for the success of the collaboration, balancing the hardcore style of Moxley with Tanahashi's more traditional puroresu approach. But it worked - and by the time Moxley's hand was raised, AEW and New Japan had a success on their hands. This all begged the question: what next? Could the two companies forge a more permanent arrangement? And if so, would that constitute a global wrestling superpower that might pose a threat to WWE?

CHAPTER 1
SLIDING DOORS
ISSUE 44, AUGUST 2022
H G MCLAREN

H G MCLAREN *examines what pro wrestling's latest supershow really means for the global grappling landscape*

When All Elite Wrestling's joint supercard with NJPW was announced in late April of this year, fans the world over salivated over the potential dream encounters which might take place. After all, the industry's two premier in-ring products combining rosters to present a never-before-seen collaboration had the very real potential to be one of the best top-to-bottom cards of all time. From old rivalries and partnerships being rekindled to highly anticipated first time ever showdowns, opening wrestling's 'Forbidden Door' now allowed smart fan fantasy booking to become a reality. It came as no surprise then that tickets for the event flew out the door, with the show's pre-sale selling out within just forty minutes.

While wrestling news sites and journalists placed their focus on what talents could appear and exactly who they might face, little attention was being given to a far wider area of intrigue. What did a public collaboration of this level between the corporation's two biggest rivals mean for World Wrestling Entertainment? As with so many things in life, as the months passed, timing was everything. Yet few could have foreseen that the opening of this 'Forbidden Door' would perfectly coincide with the opening of something else – WWE's very own Pandora's box of upper management missteps.

JUST A LITTLE BIT OF HISTORY REPEATING ITSELF

While the phenomenon really became a major talking point over the last five years, WWE gobbling up talent faster than their rivals can compete is far from new. Back before they 'got the F out', the 1980s version of wrestling's most dominant brand used almost exactly the same tactic to weaken their territorial rivals. Working at a lightning pace, Vince McMahon would make unrefusable offers to the top stars in America's major territories, all with a view to create his very own 'supercard roster' but this time, presented on a national - not regional - stage. The way to additionally jet fuel this approach was to blow the quality of everybody else's television production out of the water and then offer it to the very same stations that had been airing the same old, dated regional programming for decades – now all minus their most popular wrestlers. A masterstroke to those who benefited from it and dirty tricks to those that didn't, the only thing that all can agree on about this strategy was that it proved highly effective.

As WWF's former peers slowly drowned, desperation set in with shows like AWA's 'WrestleRock Rumble' designed as an attempt to compete with McMahon's larger than life presentation of wrestling and usurp him from his new throne as the king of sports entertainment. Whilst, on occasion, there were some strong showings from these attempts to counter program the WWF, their ultimate success can be best summed up in just one way. From AWA to World Class, all the way to

WCW – none of those companies even exist today and the supercards that they once held to battle McMahon can now be found in the archives of his own network. Game, set and match.

What Vince's competitors failed to understand back then, prior to the formation of ECW at least, was that wrestling fans cared far less about the company's name or initials and volumes more about the stars which they showcased. In short, without featuring the talent that fans really wanted to see, no amount of inventive supercards would bring viewers back to these flagging promotions - at least in the numbers they needed. With Vince showcasing his wrestlers in a bigger and better way than any promoter ever had, not to mention paying many far more than they could make elsewhere, why would said talent desire to go back to the old, dying territories? Even the support of billionaire Ted Turner struggled to make anything but a medium sized dent in the overwhelming perception at the time that WWF was number one and second best (WCW) was still many miles behind it.

PERCEPTION ISN'T ALWAYS REALITY

Apart from a slight blip that you may have heard of called 'The Monday Night Wars', this perception of WWF/E as the only place wrestlers go to say they'd 'made it' continued until very recently. Even stars like AJ Styles, Samoa Joe, Shinsuke Nakamura and KENTA described getting to WWE as their dream home, despite their vast list of prior achievements outside of it. This couldn't help but have had a ripple effect in the minds of younger wrestlers, a few rungs on the ladder below them. For talent like Styles and Joe, who had seen ECW's cult following and high quality in-ring output, ending up in a company like TNA – a better produced, more televised and financially stable WWE alternative than Paul Heyman's attempt – likely seemed fitting. However, being 'TNA originals' is not the story we'll all remember about their career. Instead, by going to WWE, along with the demise of Impact itself, it sent an altogether different message. Younger aspiring wrestlers now had just two options; the indies with the odd overseas booking chucked in or WWE.

The only thing that would have likely pushed said talent towards the former and stay 'independent', was the WWE style itself. Polished, slower and more centred on characters, the average indie standout could easily look quickly out of place in such a production, much as Joe and AJ could well have done had they signed ten years earlier. That was, of course, until WWE launched its own indie of sorts - NXT. Triple H's pet project gave those aspiring to follow in the footsteps of Joe, Nakamura and many others the chance to do so, perfecting their showmanship on killer cards prior to an eventual main roster call-up.

On paper, the NXT to WWE talent model was exceptional. It allowed new talent a place to learn, whilst also showcasing them to a very vocal section of the WWE fanbase. It provided the WWE Network a true in-house alternative for those older fans, looking for something a little more edgy. This would in turn make indie talent fans of WWE's new, trendier brand and thus, could make them more inclined to sign with them over New Japan, ROH or AAA. It also 'just happened' to drain more talent from the industry than ever before, leaving any would-be competitors to Vince McMahon's crown fighting over scraps.

That wasn't all though. With the addition of NXT:UK, coincidentally launched shortly after Great Britain got its first big budget, nationally televised wrestling brand in three decades, the WWE prepared to embark on its most ambitious venture yet – 'Global Localisation'. In many ways, it was Triple H's very own equivalent of what his father-in-law did to the US territories in the eighties. Signing the top talent in each burgeoning region to an exclusive contract but, unlike the 1980's boom, sign them not to the main brand, but to a selection of locally run satellite brands. In essence, WWE's very own 'Indie killer'.

From the outside looking in, this was just the WWE reacting to the changing fanbase and offering them something different to Raw and Smackdown. From the inside looking out, it was far more insidious than that. Still, that didn't stop booming UK stand-outs Progress Wrestling and ICW from buying in to WWE's promise of something better, despite all of their punk-rock or counter-culture rhetoric in the many years prior to signing a deal to appear on the network. Germany's WXW and America's EVOLVE would join them. The industry waited with bated breath to see what WWE's impact on the UK wrestling scene would truly be – a scene that had been experiencing its biggest boom period in almost forty years.

Unsurprisingly, the growth, excitement and record crowds that British wrestling had been experiencing in the years prior to WWE's 'intervention' ground to a sudden halt. While those deluding themselves with palms full of McMahon gold and silver might have claimed otherwise, NXT:UK did not help independent British wrestling but rather, it stunted the scene's growth immeasurably.

CALL TO ARMS

The UK would quickly become a dire warning to the rest of the wrestling world. NXT now appeared to be WWE's Trojan horse and if let through the gate, expect to see it gobble up the best parts of your entire scene. This lesson proved to be a powerful one for promoters in Japan, when WWE announced the Land of the Rising Sun as the destination for their next chapter of 'global localisation'. Similar to their model in Great Britain, WWE set about to find a willing collaborator. They settled on Pro Wrestling NOAH, once the home of some of the world's top in-ring confrontations. Largely due to Japan's code of honour and secrecy, much of what went down behind closed doors will likely remain that way for a long time, if not forever. Yet what we do know is that an attempt by WWE to buy NOAH proved unsuccessful, majorly disrupting the proposed NXT:Japan launch. Whilst thwarted, WWE's audacious plan put every company in Japan, and all over the world, on notice; they could be coming for your region next.

Perhaps Triple H had made his first major error here, though. As other powerful figures have painfully learned throughout history, nothing can destroy a powerful empire faster than fighting several wars on multiple fronts, all at once. While distracted with plans to unseat Japan's top brands under the guise of global localisation, just as they had in the UK, NXT had problems of its own. To begin with, while NXT:UK's larger events were of extremely high quality, the subsequent weekly TV was far from a critical success. Uninspiring presentation and storytelling meant that the shining light of WWE's new global strategy wasn't even ranking in the top ten most watched shows on its own network. As bad as that sounds, what was happening back home in the United States was far worse.

In the pursuit of destabilising wrestling scenes around the world, global localisation had only been successful in destabilising one thing – the original NXT itself. By placing focus on the UK and now Japan, Triple H had overlooked the only real war that his father in-law required a general to fight; the rise of AEW. This simple oversight would be the first step in the genius of NXT rapidly collapsing in on itself. With AEW regularly beating NXT on Wednesday nights, along with many of those unhappy with WWE or fired for no good reason signing with Tony Khan and making huge waves, a vital industry narrative began to shift. If legends like Chris Jericho were signing with AEW or talent like Jon Moxley and Daniel Bryan were actually leaving WWE to go there, maybe WWE was losing its hold on wrestler's hearts and minds?

However, it can also be argued that the likes of Adam Cole jumping directly from NXT sent a message of equal proportions. His defection, along with many others, proved that not only was WWE not the hip, cool brand anymore – NXT wasn't either. In an amazing act of possibly unintentional self-awareness, NXT would later rebrand itself in the least cool way possible. With more and more prominent talent picking AEW over WWE or wasted talent leaving Vince, only to get used properly by Tony Khan, something else was happening. Talent's open excitement at being 'All Elite', alongside sharing their frustrations with WWE management and creative, rapidly begun to affect fan sentiment too. Just years earlier, thanks in part to NXT, WWE had no real competition for the affection of wrestling fans. Now, nothing could be further from the truth.

STRENGTH IN NUMBERS

And so, with WWE's plan for global domination over the world's domestic scenes laid bare for all to see, it would be foolhardy for those firmly in the corporation's sights not to seize on the right moment to protect themselves. Opening the 'Forbidden Door' could be just the first step to that. With early reports indicating that the show made over $5,000,000 on pay-per-view alone, it's certainly a wake-up call to those previously reluctant to 'partner up' with their old rivals.

This concept could extend even further. By pooling resources outside of just running the odd supershow together, companies like AEW and New Japan finally have a way to change the narrative. The commonly held belief that "AEW or NJPW is where talent goes for steady pay and great artistic freedom, but WWE is where the big money and big crowds are" can finally be overturned. If a 'collaboration contract' meant that a talent had all of AEW's perks but with NJPW tours or big shows like Wrestle Kingdom thrown-in, along with the odd high-paying, overseas booking and the ability to control their own third-party revenue streams like Twitch or OnlyFans, WWE would struggle to compete for talent for the first time since WCW.

As Vince proved in the 80s and again during 'The Attitude Era', fans often go where the wrestlers do. Opening a door once forbidden, opens up something else – the door to many talents' dream career of travel, fun, artistic expression, security and… freedom. The fact that the WWE now has much bigger and well publicised problems of its own to deal with means that the timing for such high-level collaborations has never been more fortuitous. With the industry giant's aggressive plans revealed to all, whilst simultaneously now being exposed and vulnerable, the ideal strategy for AEW, NJPW and every other wrestling company is not to attack but to reinforce the battlements.

No one believes that WWE won't recover from this recent controversy, no matter how serious it looks. Yet when McMahon and co finally return their firm focus to global wrestling domination, they may just find a very different landscape existing than the one that they once knew. A landscape that, if their rivals can put business over infighting, is now almost impenetrable from future attack.

RULE OF ENGAGEMENT #12: PROMOTE YOUR BEST LIEUTENANT WHEN THE TIME IS RIGHT

The latter half of 2022 was a defining period for WWE as it witnessed a significant transformation under the creative direction of Paul 'Triple H' Levesque. Following Vince McMahon's resignation in the summer, Levesque assumed a pivotal role in shaping WWE's creative landscape - and he did so at a crucial juncture. The company, which had faced years of criticism for stagnating storylines and a perceived disconnect with its fan base, was in dire need of rejuvenation. Levesque, with his extensive experience as a performer and his successful tenure overseeing developmental brand NXT, brought a fresh perspective. His approach emphasised long-term storytelling, character development, and a renewed focus on in-ring performance.

Critically, WWE's product began to show marked improvements. Television ratings, a key metric in gauging audience interest, saw a notable uptick. For instance, Monday Night RAW's average viewership in the autumn of 2022 was approximately 10-15% higher compared to the same period in the previous year. Commercially, WWE also experienced positive trends. WWE's quarterly financial reports indicated a rise in merchandise revenue, bolstered by the popularity of newly pushed talents and refreshed character merchandise.

Live event attendance, another crucial indicator of the company's health, showed a resurgence. Cities that hosted WWE events reported higher attendance figures compared to the previous year. This was not only indicative of the growing interest in WWE's live shows but also highlighted the success of Levesque's efforts in making the live experience more engaging and appealing to fans. The good times were really starting to roll again, but little did anyone know at the time, the landscape was only months away from shifting yet again.

Street Journal published the first of its bombshell reports into the conduct of Vince McMahon.

By now anyone even vaguely interested (and probably millions more who aren't) are well aware of the allegations made against McMahon, accused of paying millions in 'hush money' payments to a string of women he had affairs with. The ethical morass created by his actions aside, McMahon now needs to worry about how the financial implications of his actions will be viewed legally.

While there may be some fallout still to come for the former WWE Chairman, things have moved on in his absence at a frightening pace. That should come as no surprise given WWE is a billion-dollar juggernaut, with shareholders, sponsors, and a global audience to appease.

THE MCMAHON-LEVESQUE ERA

What was unexpected was how quickly Stephanie McMahon and Paul Levesque, for years WWE's on-screen power couple, found themselves elevated to their loftiest positions ever in Vince's stead.

It makes for a fascinating case study in how one's standing can fluctuate over the years, seemingly as the wind blows, with regards to Levesque. Fans and wrestlers alike have been quick to react positively to the news that the 'Cerebral Assassin' will be in charge of two key areas of WWE business – talent relations and creative.

Where once these were the protected realms of Vince McMahon and perceived yes-men such as John Laurinaitis and Bruce Prichard, now the son-in-law gets his chance to try and replicate the success he found running NXT for years on the main stage. Everyone has been pretty unanimous that this is a good thing.

STILL GAME: TRIPLE H TO THE RESCUE?

Let's face it – looking at WWE purely in terms of creative direction and talent-related decisions over the past few years, things could not have got much worse.

Levesque knows what it is to be beloved, both by his fans and his employees. Thanks to his astute management (and limitless budget, among other things), NXT was a critical success which grew from a cult favourite to an internationally respected wrestling promotion. There are very few fans who did not enjoy NXT's output during its 2014-19 glory period. Fewer still are the workers in his orbit who do not owe him a debt of gratitude for furthering their careers.

The perception that Levesque had the 'Midas touch' was dealt a severe blow during the 18-month spell that NXT went head-to-head with AEW Dynamite on Wednesday nights, between 2019 and 2021. During that period, AEW was the most-watched wrestling show for 63 of 75 weeks in overall viewership, as well as generally winning in the key demographics.

The result? WWE did something it has rarely, if ever, done, and retreated. NXT was moved to Tuesday evenings, and Triple H was left to comment publicly that it was for purely strategic reasons. Meanwhile, word within WWE was that his star had fallen in Vince's eyes and was no longer viewed as the obvious successor he once seemed.

Health reasons, rather than performance, forced Levesque to step away from the business for several months late last year; while he was gone, McMahon did away with pretty much everything that 'The Game' held dear. TakeOvers? Gone. The black-and-gold? Gone. The Cruiserweight title and 205 Live? History.

Now, with Vince gone after a whirlwind couple of months, Levesque is more powerful than ever and everyone is championing him as this saviour of wrestling. It's almost too good to be true. Then again, the man who once wrestled as Hunter

Hearst Helmsley has always had a knack for landing on his feet.

CALL ME 'PAUL'

"We call him Papa H because he's been there for everything, like every part of our career, even on the main roster. Anytime we had a question, professionally, personally, he was always there for us. I think he always gave me that confidence that I needed."

Zelina Vega was effusive in her praise for Levesque when she appeared on Ryan Satin's Out of Character podcast in November. It is a sentiment shared by dozens, if not hundreds, of wrestlers and staff who have come through WWE's Performance Center to NXT to main roster pipeline in the last decade. It is not hard to grasp why.

Over the course of four decades running the WWF/WWE, Vince McMahon attained a reputation, rightly or wrongly, as a fearsome character. Someone who would tear up scripts, change plans on the fly, and recoil if someone so much as sneezed in his presence. Sure, these stories probably took on a life of their own, and plenty of top talent regarded McMahon as a father figure. Nevertheless, his status as a caustic character with scathing opinions and no time to waste was well earned.

Levesque, certainly, has been an antidote to this. The multiple-time former world champion first became an executive in WWE in 2010, focused on talent and live events, after a decade as an unofficial advisor and assistant booker. He has been responsible for spearheading WWE's talent development since becoming one of the top brass, outlining his vision to USA Today in 2015:

"I started putting together this plan in my head and [Vince] and I worked on it, and he said, 'I think this is a great thing. Go do it.'

STILL GAME: TRIPLE H TO THE RESCUE?

And that's what we've done [in NXT]. To see them go out there and knock it out of the park [on the main roster] and see how happy they are, it's awesome, man. In some ways it's like watching my kids."

We're not quite there yet, but it's presumably not long until we see Stephanie, Paul and Shane's kids wrestling for WWE. Until that time arrives, the former Triple H has cultivated a beloved status among the wrestlers who have passed through the doors of the Performance Center, taking a proud, paternal posture as 'his' boys and girls have grown and developed.

It is not just wrestlers and wannabe wrestlers that Levesque has spent the last few years charming over to his way of doing things. The one-time Connecticut Blueblood has enjoyed a very different relationship with the media than that of his father-in-law, as he encouraged questions from wrestling websites alongside traditional reporting by national and international publications.

We've not had one in a while, but media calls prior to each NXT TakeOver were a regular occurrence until last year, as Levesque would respond to softball questions in return for guaranteed publicity of his next big show. Cynics might call it a transparent attempt to curry favour, but either way, it worked wonders for both the NXT brand, and his own standing.

It wasn't always this way. For younger fans, or anyone with an understandable fondness for NXT black-and-gold, it may be hard to fathom – but Levesque knows what it's like to be hated just as much as loved.

TURN AND TURN AGAIN

Certain wrestlers turn face and heel so many times they gain a reputation for it. The obvious performer in this category is the former 'Big Show' Paul Wight. Wight acknowledged as much in a recent interview, noting that "the fans have said I've had more turns than Nascar." It's a pretty apt description for a man who played a character that changed his allegiances at a dizzying pace during his career.

While few can hold a candle to the number of turns Wight racked up, all that was purely in storyline. Behind the scenes, Paul Levesque may be a contender for someone whose reputation has risen and fallen at a similar tempo. Emotions have always seemingly run high in regard to Triple H, among the audience, the office, and fellow wrestlers. His most recent rebirth as 'main roster saviour' is simply the latest chapter in a long, confounding biography.

When you reflect upon the story of Levesque's rise, one thread sustains the narrative; namely, opportunity. When to spot it, when to expect it, when to exploit it. As will become clear, Mr Stephanie McMahon has proven time and time again to be perhaps the most politically adept operator the business of wrestling has ever seen. This in turn, has had differing impacts on how he is perceived at different times.

Simply put, he has always been able to spot an opportunity. Before he was even in the business, he had a keen sense of how to get ahead. An avid gym buff as a teen, Levesque by coincidence ended up training in the same New Haven, Connecticut gym as Ted Arcidi, a bodybuilder who had a brief wrestling career, including a stint in the WWF.

After much persuading, Arcidi connected the promising upstart with a trainer in the form of Walter "Killer" Kowalski. The old-school heel in turn showed Levesque the ropes and readied him for his first excursions on the north-east indie circuit of the early 1990s. Before long, the young hopeful had talked his way into a try-out with World Championship Wrestling (WCW), after smooth-talking the likes of then-WCW President Bob Dhue.

Despite only having a couple of years of experience in the

business at that point, Levesque was keenly aware of his potential. Operating counter to most people's instincts, the newcomer sensed it might be sensible not to get tied down too long-term to WCW and talked Eric Bischoff out of giving him a long-term contract. He explained to Loudwire in 2020:

"I was like, 'Alright, it's a multi-year deal, what if I just did one year?' And he was like, 'So I'm offering you multi-years, you just want to sign one? It's kind of a dumb decision.' I said, 'Look, here's how I look at it, let me wrestle for you for a year. At the end of the year, you're either going to know I'm worth a lot more than $52,000, or I ain't worth keeping.'"

Clearly, there was a third possibility that Bischoff had not considered – but Levesque had. The future Triple H used the Atlanta-based company as a place to get used to wrestling on television and pay-per-view, honing his craft, and wound up with interest from the industry-leading WWF. When his year was nearing its end, Levesque simply handed in his notice, much to the annoyance of Bischoff.

From there, it was off to the big-time. Levesque continued to absorb everything around him in his quest to become the best, most well-rounded pro wrestler he could be. He certainly excelled at that. What some would call spotting opportunity, others might term 'sucking up' to people in power. That was definitely the opinion of Shane Douglas, who had his own far less successful spell in the WWF in 1995. He told PowerSlam magazine the following year:

"And then there's Hunter Hearst Helmsley . . . Actually, I know why he's in The Clique. It hit me when we were on tour in Germany: he carries the bags for Diesel and Razor Ramon. He carries their bags! Now, I've done some things in this business which I'm not proud of, like being Dean Douglas and a Dynamic Dude, but I have never, ever carried anyone's bags."

In the decades since his WWF debut, it has become commonplace to accuse Triple H of buddying up to the right people – Shawn Michaels, the McMahon family, and others –

but in 1996 the accusation was pretty stark. Whether accurate or not, one thing is for sure – within months of first stepping foot into a WWF ring, Levesque was part of Michaels' inner circle; with that came the scope to influence WWF honcho Vince McMahon, something he would make a lifestyle out of.

ONE NIGHT IN MONTREAL

Levesque was not always in the good books in Stamford, Connecticut of course. He was punished, briefly, for his part in the overblown 'Curtain Call' incident by missing out on pay-per-view bookings for a bit; but the plan was always to push him strong. It is a favourite factoid of many that Helmsley was due to win the 1996 King of the Ring. Instead, he had to settle with the Intercontinental title four months later. Not too shabby.

Throughout his formative Federation years, the public reception to Levesque was one of apathy. While his in-ring work was serviceable, his gimmick greatly limited him. That started to change in 1997, and once again it was thanks to being in the orbit of Shawn Michaels.

With no real storyline, Helmsley and Chyna began accompanying main eventer Michaels in August 1997 (despite the fact that he already had his own kayfabe bodyguard in Rick Rude). No attempt was made to explain why this 'Connecticut Blueblood' and the 'Boy Toy' were suddenly best mates. It was simply the two transposing their behind-the-scenes friendship onto television.

Levesque may have been the junior partner to Michaels in their backstage meddling at the time, but he certainly knew how to influence people. In hindsight it seems a cast of thousands were involved in plotting to remove the WWF Title

STILL GAME: TRIPLE H TO THE RESCUE?

from Bret Hart at Survivor Series '97, and we can be pretty certain Triple H had his say.

Various players have come forward in the years since to detail their involvement, with at least one account suggesting it was Levesque, in his role as Michaels' best friend, who suggested the WWF take matters into its own hands as it pertained to Hart's uncooperative stance.

The drama that followed was documented memorably in *Wrestling With Shadows*. In it, Levesque has a miniscule but notable cameo. Moments after the screwjob has taken place, Bret's wife Julie Hart is in the bowels of the arena, making it clear that she suspects foul play. Levesque looks at the ground like a scolded schoolboy as he claims, unconvincingly, to know nothing about it. Hart, nobody's fool, laments:

"Yeah, well swear to God all you want. Some day God is going to strike you down."

For many wrestling fans with long memories, Levesque's involvement, and hang-dog expression when called out, set a course for what to expect from him over the years. To millions more though, he has been a hero.

PERFECT TIMING

By the spring of 1998, Levesque's trajectory had skyrocketed, thanks in large part to the circumstances around him; namely, the departure of Hart and the enforced absence of Michaels. As the authority-defying leader of D-X Mark II Triple H became an indelible part of what became known as the Attitude Era.

Fans warmed to Triple H over the next 18 months as he was prepped for a proper main event run alongside the best cast in wrestling history, rubbing shoulders on a weekly basis with the likes of Steve Austin, The Rock, The Undertaker and

Mankind. When he lifted his first WWF world title, the jury was still out on if he had what it took to stay the course as an engaging main eventer. Levesque proved any doubters wrong, even if his importance to that halcyon era is at times overstated.

Fortune smiled on Levesque again in 2001 – although it probably didn't feel fortunate at the time. On the May 21th episode of *Raw*, Triple H tore a quadriceps muscle during a scintillating tag match against Chris Benoit and Chris Jericho. That type of injury can be excruciating and posed a threat to Levesque's long-term ability to perform.

The element of luck was two-fold. Firstly, it meant "The Game" missed the entire WCW Invasion angle from start to finish. Indeed, the first run-in (by Lance Storm) took place on the very next Monday. While Helmsley would have been assured a top spot and protected throughout, the angle was a messy one and it ended up being a situation which increased his stock by being absent for it.

The long lay-off also made Levesque the beneficiary of that old adage – 'absence makes the heart grow fonder.' Nothing pleases a wrestling fan more than a surprise debut or return. And if it's one that feels like it might have a wider significance, even better. That is exactly what we got at the 2002 Royal Rumble when Triple H made his glorious return at Madison Square Garden. The eight-month recuperation. The doubt. The iconic venue. The crowd went ballistic. Truly, he had arrived. He later told ESPN:

"It was great. You know, it's hard to put into words the journey that I was on at this point in time because there was a high probability that I would never wrestle again with the injury that I had, and they kind of let me know that. So, coming back, having the return that I did and having the opportunity to do that at Madison Square Garden, and the reaction and everything was incredible."

. . .

ONE OF THE FAMILY

If you didn't know better, looking back at the reaction that night might give you the impression that this was the jumping off point for Levesque to become one of the most beloved babyfaces of all time. Far from it. Triple H, a natural heel if there ever was one, was ever-present in WWE for the next decade, usually at the top of the card, often holding a world title, and pretty much always the villain.

With Levesque as WWE's top heel, life began to imitate art once more, as rumours and stories of his outsized backstage influence swirled throughout the noughties. That decade brought almost unparalleled success inside the ring, such as 14 world titles, WrestleMania main events and much more.

For many, the reason for Levesque's staying power during the first decade of the century was obvious – his 2003 marriage to the bosses' daughter and his ability to sway Vince McMahon to his point of view. Clearly, that is an oversimplification, but it certainly helped. When Hunter wasn't being handed world championships for no particular reason (as Eric Bischoff did in 2002), he was facing – and usually beating – anyone who could threaten his spot.

A lot is made of psychology in wrestling. One very simple aspect of this is that, eventually, the heel loses. A heel can go on a rampage, amass victory after victory, and get booked like a monster. But there is only one reason for that – to eventually put over a babyface in convincing fashion and transfer their momentum to the real top guy.

This was famously not something Triple H was keen on. Instead, he preferred to have his cake and eat it; to be the cool, cocky bad guy, but also to bulldoze everyone in sight without often having to put people over unless he absolutely had to. To his credit, he did put over Benoit, Batista and Cena in consecutive 'Mania main events to aid the company in building new stars.

The list of those who benefitted from Triple H's rub is a short one. Much longer is the roll call of people who might have benefited if Levesque had not seen the need to steamroll them quite so decisively. For the second time in his career, after the mid-90s antics of the Clique impacted those around it, Levesque gained a reputation for burying others for his benefit. Rob Van Dam, Jeff Hardy, Booker T and others all came a cropper when 'The Game' deemed them not worthy of his full commitment.

MR INDEPENDENT

Levesque's tendency to undermine opponents was not confined to the ring. A famous tale which did the rounds in 2005 relates to the current head of WWE creative and talent relations appraising the debuting CM Punk. Punk had arrived as an indie favourite, which clearly meant little to Triple H.

The story goes that he, Michaels and Michael Hayes watched Punk's match on a monitor and were scathing about what they saw – all agreeing with each other that the new signing didn't know 'how to work'. This was far from the only time Levesque would claim this about a new face, with his ire particularly savage towards stars of the independent circuit.

Speaking on Gerweck Radio in 2013, former WWE tag team champion Paul London noted:

"Hunter was pretty obviously jealous of certain individuals. I'm not saying he was jealous of me. I could tell he was envious of (Rob) Van Dam. He was extremely envious of Rob's success. He was jealous of Van Dam's personality. He was jealous that people gravi-

tated towards Rob, because people liked being around Rob because he was very positive."

An element of workplace friction is to be expected wherever you go. Over the last quarter of a century, it seems Levesque has made a habit of exploiting his leverage when these personal frictions arise. It is that kind of sentiment people would be wise to bear in mind when proclaiming him as the second coming. Levesque has also allowed himself the luxury of airing his prejudices in worked-shoot promos, as he did on Raw in 2013:

"I've seen guys like you come and go a million times. Guys like Jericho, Edge, Rob Van Dam. All guys that are very talented, don't get me wrong. Top guys! Very popular! But not 'the one.' Never were they 'the one.' And maybe nobody wants to say this, but it needs to be said: It's a fact. If any of those guys had been the face of the WWE back in the day, we'd all be working for Ted Turner right now."

As Chris Jericho promptly observed on Twitter later that night – Triple H was never the absolute top guy either, despite his prolonged, generous push. The themes that start to recur are prejudice, and opportunity. The latter of those sentiments won out in the early 2010s, as Levesque seemingly put aside his issues with indie talent, signing them up in droves as he sought to build his own promotion. In the eyes of many, it is his crowning achievement.

After spending his entire wrestling career diminishing the talents of anyone from the indie scene, Levesque started recruited them in his droves when he took over WWE's farm league. By 2012, WWE's developmental strategy was rudderless since Vince McMahon had mostly stopped caring. Triple H carefully curated NXT – the 'black-and-gold' era – and it was a critical success.

This led to Levesque becoming more popular with hardcore wrestling fans than ever before. It was not just fans either; in 2015, for his efforts with NXT, Levesque was named booker of the year by the Wrestling Observer Newsletter, not an achievement to be sniffed at.

Behind the scenes, he worked wonders too. The first inklings that he could be The Great Redeemer came when he mended the bridges that brought Bruno Sammartino and Warrior back to WWE. Where his father-in-law was all 'Scorched Earth' and vindictiveness, Triple H saw the value in being mature and conciliatory...if it served him a purpose, of course.

Over in NXT, every TakeOver was a smash; the weekly shows were great; every new star got over; fans were engaged and absorbed. This was a time when it seemed like the good times would never end for NXT and, by extension, Triple H. Not quite.

Many people interpreted Levesque's smart stewardship of NXT as a practice run for how well he would do when he inevitably, eventually took charge of WWE. For people of a more pessimistic disposition, it was not quite so simple.

NXT circa 2012 to 2018 was a great training ground for Triple H as a booker, for sure. But it also had numerous advantages that no other booker up to that point had ever benefited from. Limitless budget; no pressure to garner television ratings; an evolving cast with no chance of acts getting stale; no interference from the top boss; the promise of a promotion to an even bigger show if talent does well. In truth, NXT was fantasy land. A promotion scientifically grown in a lab for success. It is not a realistic template for anything.

There were side effects. Levesque became the global leader in stockpiling talent. His desire to have a never-ending conveyor belt of interesting new surprises meant the indie scene was gutted, especially in the UK. Ring of Honor went out of business, and the British wrestling scene shows no sign of recovery.

Meanwhile, in chasing what was essentially a vanity project, Levesque lost sight of what NXT was supposed to be

– developmental. Act after act from NXT failed to ignite on WWE's main roster. Vince McMahon may be more to blame for that, but Levesque should have known better than to ignore what attributes equalled success on the main stage. He spent enough of his career criticising those who he believed lacked the tools to prosper at the highest level.

When McMahon needed an obstacle to throw in the path of the upstart All Elite Wrestling in October 2019, finally he took an interest in NXT. The show was thrust onto the USA Network and promptly endured 18 months of ratings misery at the hands of its new rival. Levesque was not used to losing and it started to show. His usually congenial manner started to elude him, going so far as to criticise fans in one media call in 2021:

"How about watch it? Do you like it, or do you not like it? Do you have to say, 'I like it, but I like this other thing more,' or 'I like it, but I don't like it as much as I like that one.' Just watch it or don't and stop trying to figure out where everything goes."

From hero, steering NXT to critical acclaim, to zero. With the shine well and truly off NXT, and in Vince McMahon's bad books, if the rumours at the time were to be believed. Illness forced Levesque into a long lay-off last year and he sat on the side-lines with his reputation in question, if not in tatters. No longer was he the heir apparent. No longer was he the automatic replacement many had assumed he would be. What exactly was he?

SINCE YOU'VE BEEN GONE

Shawn Michaels was left in charge of NXT in Triple H's absence. He has claimed that reports of Vince and Bruce Prichard's influence have been overstated, but one thing we can be certain of is that all hallmarks of Levesque's NXT were scrubbed from existence. The name, the colour scheme, the tone – all of it was booted from September 2021 – right down to Bron Breakker destroying the old logo live on air. You can't get much more symbolic than that.

After months away, Levesque returned to apparently lighter duties, before his wife took an abrupt leave of absence, to make matters even less clear. Before anyone could blink, Vince was out, Stephanie was back (alongside Nick Khan) in full charge of the business, and Triple H has been gifted his two favourite sandpits to play in – talent relations and creative.

Something that for years looked incredibly likely, then very unlikely, has been thrust upon us with next to no warning. Triple H has soared to power. Predictably, the minor yet astute changes he has instituted on the main roster have been met with acclaim and he is once more being championed as the saviour of professional wrestling.

Everyone has had their say. WWE talents new and old have lined up around the block to talk in interviews about how great Levesque is as a leader; how reasonable he is. The sub-text of course is that Vince McMahon was anything but. Plenty of this praise needs to be viewed in context as exactly what you would expect from subordinates, or others keen to keep on his good side. But the level of praise has been quite something. Clearly, WWE could not get much worse under the previous regime.

As if by magic, everything is perfect for Levesque, more powerful than ever before, and he is back to being everyone's babyface. And just like that…everything is fine again, apparently. Better than fine. Who would have thought it? One of the worst scandals to hit WWE. Could it bizarrely be the best thing to ever happen to the company?

To hear some tell it, Triple H has arrived with his magic wand, to hire the people you want hired, to loosen up what terminology can be used, and to just generally be sensible. To cater for wrestling fans. Novel concept, eh? Like a Disney fairy changing things back to how they should be, and everyone waking up from a long sleep, a big fat kiss of life has been placed on the lips of the sleeping beauty of pro wrestling and we're all set to live happily ever after. Surely there is more to it than this?

The possibilities are endless, or so some think. Sasha Banks and Bray Wyatt will surely return, if they haven't already by the time you read this. Doudrop might get a better name. Shotzi will get her tank back. HHH knows how to push wrestling fans' buttons and give them what they want. He can read people like a book – it's one of his great strengths.

Want Pete Dunne back? No problem. Want Ali to get a push? Sure thing. It all feels a bit too good to be true. The first two months of the Levesque regime were punctuated by the returns of several former NXT talents, in the form of Dakota Kai, Hit Row, and Johnny Gargano, and others. But what is the point of bringing these people back? Who actually missed Ashanti Adonis? As Levesque has already proven, fan service can only get you so far if there is no long-term plan behind it.

Running a wrestling company is not easy, as Tony Khan is starting to find out. Egos run rampant and smooth talk and promises only gets you so far. Even the most agreeable people can run aground under pressure. And Levesque has a mean, petty edge to him that people often forget during the good times.

From thoughtless comments about Paige and Chyna over the years, needless jabs at AEW, to doing little to address an alleged culture of bullying in developmental years ago, Triple H is a man who shines during the good times. Moments of strife might draw something quite different out of him.

So…a case of 'meet the new boss, same as the old boss'? Perhaps, after all, unsubstantiated murmurings of contract tampering were heard in August when new faces started appearing on the new roster. That's certainly a bygone Vince tactic from the territory days. Levesque immediately leaned into a number of McMahon tropes – invasions, call ups, debuts, surprises; as well as the potential folly of signing too many people (a criticism also levelled at Khan).

Triple H, from heel to face to heel to face, back to rescue us from boring episodes of Raw and SmackDown? We're all here for it. Can it duplicate the success of NXT's highest points? Perhaps – but Levesque will need to learn to curb the instincts which have curtailed his hopes in the past. If he can do that, we will all benefit – not just him.

RULE OF ENGAGEMENT #13: DO NOT TOLERATE ANY INFIGHTING AMONG YOUR TROOPS

June's Forbidden Door success happened at a time when AEW's most high profile signing was on the injured list - but by September CM Punk was back, and soon enough the summer felt like it was much more than one season ago. At the company's next pay-per-view, 'All Out', a decent on-air outing was immediately overshadowed by an incident that rapidly gained notoriety in the wrestling world. The catalyst for what came to be known as 'Brawl Out' was a media scrum held immediately after the show. The ever-outspoken Punk, sat next to Tony Khan, used the occasion to deliver an explosive and unfiltered outburst during the conference with barbs directed at several AEW personnel, including Colt Cabana, Hangman Adam Page, and crucially, The Elite—Kenny Omega and The Young Bucks (Matt and Nick Jackson). Punk's remarks were laced with personal grievances and professional frustrations, indicating deep-seated issues within AEW's locker room and exposing a divide between Punk and certain factions within the company.

Following the press conference, tensions escalated rapidly, leading to a physical altercation backstage that involved CM Punk, his associate Ace Steel, and members of The Elite.

Details of the scuffle vary, but reports suggest that the altercation was both verbal and physical, with accusations of unprofessional conduct on all sides. The incident took place in the presence of several AEW staff and wrestlers, and in its aftermath AEW took swift action. Tony Khan launched an internal investigation into the incident, as a result of which CM Punk and Ace Steel were suspended indefinitely, with their future in the company uncertain. Similarly, Kenny Omega and The Young Bucks faced suspensions for their role in the altercation. Pat Buck, Christopher Daniels, Michael Nakazawa, and Brandon Cutler were all handed suspensions too, although these were lifted when it emerged that they had all been trying to break up the fight.

So, Khan had acted swiftly - but what next? Punk was his world champion, and the Elite were the world trios champions. Those titles both had to be vacated, which obviously had an impact on creative plans. But more crucially, it now seemed clear that the company's executive vice presidents couldn't co-exist with the company's biggest star. This was a story that surely wasn't over while everyone involved remained on the payroll...

CHAPTER 3
BRAWL OUT
ISSUE 46, DECEMBER 2022
H G MCCLAREN

H G MCCLAREN *looks deeper into the latest huge news story to hit 2022 and looks at some previously unexplored links to a major story from wrestling's past...*

On October 26th, WrestleTalk hosts Oli Davis and Pete Quinnell sat down to record a YouTube video as part of a new debate format. Despite a variety of wrestling topics on offer, thanks to 2022's almost impossible to comprehend news cycle, there was only one story on most viewers minds. No, it wasn't former AEW founder Cody Rhodes jumping ship, back to the company that he only recently appeared to be hell bent on destroying – WWE. That's seemingly old news now. It wasn't Vince McMahon being forced to leave the promotion that he'd spent four decades taking to heights never seen in pro wrestling prior. The news cycle had seemingly already moved on from that too. The death and rebirth of the black and gold NXT brand, or the closure of its UK equivalent NXTUK, WWE's first tangible stab at 'global localisation', are fairly huge stories on their own. Yet, in 2022, these too appear to have been forgotten in just a matter of weeks. Perhaps, Triple H finally getting the creative reigns of the world's largest sports entertainment powerhouse, changing fan perception of the onscreen product almost instantly and ushering back use of the word 'wrestling' to WWE programming, was worth the sole focus of a fiery debate? Once more, you'd have been wrong again. That's because as the calendar rapidly approached the final quarter of arguably the craziest year our industry has seen in decades – if not ever – there was really only one topic that was setting the internet ablaze. That story was the fallout from AEW's All-Out media scrum and the alleged real life backstage altercation which followed it.

When CM Punk sat next to Tony Khan in front of a room of reporters, late in the evening of September 4th, few could have imagined what would follow. Nor could they have conceived that the words which Punk uttered next would have more of a lasting impact on All Elite Wrestling than anything which took place on the fifteen-match card before it. In fact, it wouldn't be too controversial to state that what transpired during this media scrum may end up having more of a lasting impact on AEW than any individual match to have taken place in the promotion ever. It's also a statement like this, polarising as it may be to those who disagree with its hyperbolic nature, which made for a great WrestleTalk debate.

In one corner was Oli Davis, a man who's called CM Punk his favourite wrestler publicly for many years. He's also the person who made the phrase 'CM Punk to AEW confirmed' an online meme. In many ways, Punk signing to All Elite was a validation of Davis's fandom, bringing him to tears on the WrestleTalk livestream of his hero's debut. Those tears created a clip that, due to their obvious genuine sentiment, also went viral. It should come as no surprise then, that Davis debated firmly on the side of CM Punk. Taking the opposite viewpoint was Pete Quinell. A fan of Punk's work, but not someone who was willing to turn a blind eye to what he referred to as Punk's 'toxic attitude backstage'. To Oli and Pete, the debate was simple. Does Tony Khan overlook CM Punk's wrongdoing in order to salvage a relationship with arguably the company's biggest box office attraction? It's a debate that most fans and industry insiders alike could likely pick a side on.

Yet, what if there is a far larger story underneath all of this, outside of just focusing on the current narrative alone? Furthermore, what if everything we are witnessing almost perfectly parallels another wrestling tale from the past. No, not some, hidden, obscure tale of smoke-filled rooms and 'wrasslin', but rather, one of the industry's most infamous ever. The saga of Bret Hart, Shawn Michaels and The Kliq. Perhaps by fully understanding what these parallels from the past are, we can aim to get a better grasp of the how AEW's current situation might playout in the long run. Additionally, we might also unearth a discovery far more important; how wrestling fan's changing attitudes may have just as big a part to play in all this, than any one individual alone.

THE MORE THINGS CHANGE...

In some ways, it seems almost unbelievable that this should have occurred as pro wrestling celebrated the twenty-fifth anniversary of the 'Montreal Screw Job'. So much emphasis has been placed on what took place in the ring that night in Canada, along with the screw job's eventual fallout, that younger fans could be mistaken into thinking the build-up to what happened at the Survivor Series 1997 was far less interesting. Nothing could be further from the truth. The screw job was the logical implosion of a long series of volatile events. Events which happen to bare an uncanny resemblance to CM Punk's issue with AEW's Executive Vice Presidents.

Few readers would likely welcome a long, step-by-step re-telling of either the most famous real-life rivalry of the Attitude Era (Bret versus Shawn) or AEW's most viral news story

- at least since Punk's original signing to the company. With so much written about each elsewhere, doing so again would be to re-tread a very worn path. Yet, what few wrestling media outlets, if any, have done, is to look at a side-by-side comparison of the two situations and assess their very clear connections.

It should also be noted that unlike the issues between Hart and Michaels, much of what anybody claims to know about AEW's recent backstage troubles are speculation at best. At worst, such claims are agenda laced propaganda, put out by one or more of the parties involved, likely in a hope to muddy the waters. More on that later. Being a full quarter of a century ago now, the Hart/Michaels story has been fully explored, dissected, and analysed for several decades. Since the feud between two of WWE's greatest stars of all-time 'got real', every directly affected party, indirectly involved witness or mere bystander have been interviewed exhaustively. This is not yet the case with CM Punk and AEW's 'Elite'. Although you can be fairly certain that such 'tell all' books, podcasts and shoot interviews are set to become part of wrestling's future – they do not exist yet at present. As such, much of what follows is based on second, and even third, hand accounts and opinions. To really know any of it for sure, we'll likely have to wait upon the ever-turning hands of time. Disclaimer out of the way, it is fair to class what is written next as a series of reasonable observations and logical assumptions. All of which are based on well documented, historical evidence relating to an almost identical chain of events in another wrestling promotion, at another time.

TWO TWEET

. . .

By all accounts, CM Punk and The Young Bucks were extremely friendly with each other, if not friends. Even before the formation of All Elite Wrestling, 'The Bucks' were vocal proponents of bringing the former WWE champion back into the squared circle. In August of 2017, Matt Jackson, who was part of ROH and New Japan at the time, tagged the Chicago native into a tweet displaying a Punk themed Bullet Club t-shirt which he'd designed. The brother tag team would continue to be vocal about Punk returning to wrestling in the lead-up to AEW's formation and beyond. Punk would occasionally acknowledge their tweets and comments, prior to his eventual signing with Tony Khan's brand. Many believed that Matt and Nick Jackson had played some role in making that signing happen. From the outside looking in at least, Punk and 'The Elite' were on good terms, and potentially supporters of each other. This type of friendship is something that is also often forgotten about Bret Hart and Shawn Michaels for the majority of their WWF's careers – at least before the events which lead to Montreal. In fact, the two WWE hall of famers were so close that they conspired to 'work the boys' into thinking that their bubbling rivalry had turned into a shoot. As has been the case with many worked shoots of the past, it was an agreement which would have negative consequences for all involved.

It's almost impossible to discuss Bret Hart and Shawn Michaels issues without also talking about 'The Kliq'. Much like 'The Elite', Michaels and his group of friends were believed to hold undue influence within the company they were meant to work for. This caused many wrestlers, who were not on the best terms with The Kliq, to later claim that their careers were harmed because of the group. In fact, multiple accounts claim the The Kliq's power within the company was so great, that several wrestlers had their pushes stopped and were even fired on the group's say so. Many of those most affected waited years before they told their stories, likely until they were no longer able to be affected by The Kliq's alleged undue influence. Yet, this didn't stop the rumour mill at the time from accurately 'predicting' such backstage politicking was taking place behind the scenes in WWF. There is an old industry saying, which directly relates to why such rumours always seem to surface in pro wrestling; telephone, telegram, tell a wrestler – the three fastest ways to disseminate information. As such, much like the rumours about The Kliq in the mid 90's, it is interesting to see similar ones surface presently about The Elite and their own political powerplays in AEW.

Unlike The Kliq however, The Elite's influence with Tony Khan is no secret, with many of the group being made EVPs during the company's initial formation. A title that Michaels and his crew would surely have loved back when they were busy, covertly directing the inner workings of the most powerful wrestling promotion in the world. Secondly, The Elite have certainly not been shy in giving multiple nods to The Kliq and its key members, parroting several of their sayings, hand gestures and mannerisms. It's a comparison which a wrestling historian would likely have advised The Elite to avoid continuing. Well, that's unless their aim was to remind AEW's roster members where the power to create or end talent's pushes truly lay.

In fact, in July of 2021, Matt and Nick Jackson used their Twitter bio to address the rumours of Daniel Bryan and CM Punk's imminent AEW debuts. The text merely read; "Are the rumours true? Idk. We just hope they'll take our finishes well". This was clearly meant in jest. Yet once again to those in the know, it appeared to parody The Kliq and the attitude that so many past wrestlers found themselves on the wrong end of. While this type of humour is fine at the indie level, as AEW continues to grow, being 'too sweet' for their own good may just come back to haunt the company's Executive Vice Presidents. All it would take are a few former AEW wrestlers to leave the promotion, claiming to be the victims of The Elite's toxic influence on their careers. At such point, inside jokes such as this, could create a trail of digital breadcrumbs, leading fans and journalists to believe that the comparisons between The Kliq and The Elite didn't just stop at hand gestures. It's certainly food for thought, as is the term 'hiding in plain sight'.

WORDS OF WAR

Another pivotal part of the Hart/Michaels saga was the infamous "Sunny days", comment. As most readers will know, 'The Heartbreak Kid' alluded to 'The Hitman' having an affair with WWE's first ever diva, Sunny. It was a way, at least in the storyline, for Shawn to 'confront' Bret with the accusation of being a hypocrite – preaching that he was an upstanding role model on-screen, but 'doing the dirty' on his wife when the cameras were switched off. Ironically, over a decade later, Sunny would admit that it was in fact Michaels himself that was having some 'sunny days' at the time. That being as it may, Hart claimed that the comment caused real life issues in his marriage and had no idea that Michaels would 'go there', and especially not on live television. Many on the ground at the time consider this to be the exact moment that their 'worked shoot' became far more shoot than work. It's a further bizarre coincidence then that a very similar situation is true of CM Punk's issues with The Elite.

When Adam Page decided to deviate from the agreed script in an on-air promo designed to build to his match with Punk at 'Double or Nothing', a line was certainly crossed. Much like Michaels did several decades earlier, Page brought up the personal issues between Punk and his former best friend Colt Cabana. He claimed that these issues proved

Punk, much like Bret Hart was accused of being over two decades prior, was a hypocrite. Detailing what he believed to be Punk using his leverage in AEW to prevent Cabana from being pushed within the company, Page said, "you claim to be for worker's rights, but you've done nothing but the opposite since arriving here". Punk clearly looked surprised by the line, as did fans. Some believed that this was the beginning of a work shoot angle or the seeds for a Punk heel turn. Yet, as the weeks went by, viewers started to realise that it was neither. For reasons known only to him, Hangman had 'gone into business for himself'. Or, at least so everyone would momentarily believe.

Then in August, just a month before fists would allegedly fly backstage, Punk did something strange. In a promo to set up for his world title unification match with Jon Moxley, Punk issued an open challenge to Page for an impromptu match there and then. The crowd were instantly into it. For the briefest of moments, it appeared as though Page's prior 'shoot comments' were indeed part of an elaborate storyline. Punk sat down mid-ring, as the AEW faithful prepared for the long-awaited re-match between the two. Yet what followed was one of the first times in wrestling TV history where a challenged wrestler didn't come straight through the curtain, complete with entrance music. No, in this instance – nothing happened. For a second time running, a promo involving Punk or Page had left viewers baffled. Answers were soon to follow. At least, that is, for those with a keen eye on wrestling news websites, as AEW choose not to address any of it. As it turned out, Punk's impromptu challenge was a receipt. Payback for Page's unplanned words against him prior. Suddenly, insiders began to sense this was the beginning of far larger issues for All Elite Wrestling in the months to come. Just how much larger those issues would eventually become by the following month, nobody could have predicted.

As soon as CM Punk started talking to journalists at the All Out post show media scrum, it was obvious that something was off. Having been watched millions of times on YouTube just weeks after taking place, there is no need to dissect everything he said here. In fact, the website of esteemed publication Forbes quoted just one sentence from Punk in their article detailing what the headline described as an 'ugly, profanity-laced shoot' - "I work with a bunch of f**king children". While breaking Punk's verbal tirade down into such a simplistic overview may miss many of his points, it does at least serve to underpin his prevailing mindset. While he didn't narrow focus to any one person or persons solely, most knew exactly where Punk's anger was directed: AEW's EVPs. What made the rant even more troubling, was that Tony Khan, owner of the company and Punk's boss, just sat there. In fact, clearly taken unaware by it, Khan started nodding and grinning, unsure of what to say or do as his top drawing star publicly let rip on the inner workings of his promotion. If Punk's issues where truly a lack of adult leadership at the top of AEW, exposing Khan in this way only served to highlight his concerns further – whether intentional or not.

THE BED YOU MADE

Khan himself is no stranger to 'shooting' on people both during interviews and online – especially if he disagrees with someone's views on how AEW is run. He's also not afraid to make controversial statements, which some may consider petty, arrogant or ill advised. This is something which has led to he and Eric Bischof having a long standing war of words across social media and several podcasts for over a year. It should also be noted that the 'media scrum' concept is something which many wrestling fans first became familiar with through the UFC. Punk is a former UFC fighter, intimately knowing their media game all too well. In these UFC scrums, company owner Dana White would sit next to his fighters, giving journalists much to write about, thanks to his regular off the cuff outbursts and 'profanity-laced shoots' of his own – often ranting about fighter politics, public fall outs and calling BS on journalists. With all this in mind, it should be of little surprise that an AEW media scrum would become home to something like this eventually.

And then there is CM Punk himself. As the author of 'The pipe promo', few are as fluent, succinct, and cutting on the mic. Especially when blurring the lines between fact and fiction or breaking down the 'fourth wall'. For Hangman Page to have chosen Punk to be the target of a shoot promo on television without his prior knowledge and expect no verbal retaliation, was at best a major miscalculation. At worst, it could be viewed as intentional provocation. Furthermore, the company was aware of such a situation existing and handed Punk a live mic at a 'shoot' press conference. Did the owner of the company, sat by his side, at least call a temporary halt to proceedings as soon as Punk started crossing the line? Not at all. At some points, Khan even looked like he was agreeing. With all of this in mind, it's extremely hard to claim that the blame for this lays squarely at Punk's feet alone.

BRAWL FOR ALL

With so much historical focus being placed on the Survivor Series in Montreal just a few months later, readers would be excused for not knowing the significance of June 6th, 1997. That was the date when tensions between Bret Hart and Shawn Michaels reached boiling point, leading to a backstage fight. Hart confronted Michaels about the personal problems the 'sunny days' comment had caused him at home. In 2020, on his 'Grilling JR' podcast, AEW commentator Jim Ross described the incident as follows. "It wasn't a fight that saw teeth knocked out and broken noses and eyes swelled shut and things of that nature. It didn't get that extreme, but it was intense".

The incident led to Michaels apparently slamming a clump of his hair (which had been pulled out during the fight) onto Vince McMahon's desk, claiming that the WWF had become an 'unsafe working environment'. A line that would live in wrestling infamy thanks to Jim Cornette, who worked in company management at the time, recounting Shawn's words unsympathetically on multiple occasions. The lack of sympathy displayed by Cornette was shared by many in the WWF locker room at the time. By and large, many of the company's roster felt that Michaels had it coming, as a result of The Kliq's ever-present political skulduggery. Most fans who knew about the fight at the time tended to agree, as did the majority of those who learned about it for the first time in the decades that followed. This support for Bret Hart will become important later.

It will come as little surprise to anyone what comes next, when comparing the obvious parallels between Bret and Shawn's physical altercation to AEW's. Shortly after Punk's All Out 'media pipebomb', members of The Elite entered his locker room and a brawl ensued – now aptly dubbed by journalists and fans, 'brawl out'. Accounts of what really happened vary wildly, as each side have attempted to put out their own narrative via the wrestling press in the month that followed. This includes a report from Dave Meltzer claiming that The Young Bucks believe that Punk's actions have created... wait for it... an 'unsafe working environment'. Yes, the depth of synchronicity with WWF's backstage tensions in 1997 continues. Indeed, there is only one missing element and it's one that we'll also likely never get now. This element is 97's grand finale – The Montreal Screw Job. Or, perhaps, we have already seen it and not realised?

TURNING THE SCREW

Stripped down to its most base level, what happened to make Montreal such an important part of wrestling history, was really nothing to do with Bret and Shawn. Both stars had decided to put their differences aside for the sake of the match and as such, had a fantastic encounter - save for what occurred in the final moments. The real story of Montreal is about how WWF's owner decided to act in the fallout from the rivalry between his two biggest stars. WWF's retelling of history is quick to focus on only one narrative; the story of how Vince McMahon was forced to screw Bret, in order to save the company from Hart turning up on WCW television with WWF's world title. It's a fictional scenario which many have since debunked, not least of all because of an ongoing lawsuit at the time, preventing Eric Bischoff from doing any such thing ever again. In truth, what went down in Montreal happened because McMahon had decided to back Michaels over Hart, long before they eventually locked horns at the Survivor Series. After all, 'The Hitman' wouldn't have even been leaving for WCW if McMahon hadn't requested to back out of their historic multi-decade contract, and actively asked Hart to reach out to 'the competition' and jump ship. Bret Hart did not screw the WWF – the WWF screwed Bret.

As of the time of writing, AEW's investigation into where the blame lays in 'brawl out' has not reached its final verdict – at least publicly. As the investigation, the various suspensions or even the fight which created them have yet to be acknowledged by AEW officially, it's possible that said verdict will remain private forever. Yet, as has been the case with much of this story, along with many elements which word count limitations prevented covering, certain members of the wrestling media appear to already know what's been decided. Interestingly, this consistent leaking of narratives, favourable only to certain factions of AEW, is something else that Punk alluded to, in his media scrum tirade. Strange, huh? Irrespective of that, it appears as though Tony Khan has picked a side. According to multiple reports, CM Punk's days in AEW are over.

With his air of general impatience, frosty attitude and razor-sharp tongue, Punk is extremely well suited for being painted as a villain. In fact, few wrestlers have done less to try and be liked in the sport's history - even when they were billed as a babyface. In many ways, both Phil Brooks and the character he has created are easy to dislike as, for all intents and purposes, they appear to be one and the same. However, there's an important distinction to be made. Just because someone is easy to dislike, it's doesn't mean that they are without virtue or instantly the wrong doer in every situation. On the contrary, Punk has often shown himself to be a man of principle, moral fibre and integrity in the face of injustice – no matter how big the foe he opposes. It is these traits, along with his incredible talent and self-belief, which made fans in arenas all over the world chant his name, almost as a protest vote against a wrestling empire which was falling short of expectations – the voice of the voiceless, no less. Perhaps, Punk is doing the same thing at this very moment, no matter how unpopular it might be to hear?

SHOOT TO KILL

As the 1990's faded into a new millennium, a unique wrestling format found its way into the lives of fans – the shoot interview. For the first time ever, lovers of the squared circle could hear all about the inner workings of the industry, through the unfiltered and often outspoken views of the men and women who were on the inside. It was via these early videos that stories of The Kliq's backstage tendencies and the 'truth' about Bret and Shawn's issues would be etched into the annals of wrestling folklore forever. These revelations led many a fan who'd grown up cheering Michaels, Scott Hall and Kevin Nash, to now see them as the real-life heels of that era. It was also a stink that lingered on fellow Kliq member Triple H all the way up to the formation of NXT. A brand which some believe he created purely to win over the army of vocal critics he'd acquired, due in no small part to his involvement in The Kliq's treatment of Bret Hart. It was also these shoot interviews that paved the way for many fans to become 'smart', opening the door for a company like AEW to even exist in the first place.

How strange might it feel then, if the shoot interviews of the future also paint an alternative version of what's happening in AEW right now? A story where history really has repeated itself once again, and where CM Punk isn't just one man with a bad attitude rocking an otherwise happy boat? Lest we forget that not long before this, the biggest story in wrestling was Cody Rhodes leaving the company that he'd helped found (AEW), only to return to its biggest rival. At the time, much of wrestling media framed Rhodes as a sell out and, you guessed it, a hypocrite. Yet, considering what's recently been accused by Punk, isn't it prudent to at least ponder if where there is smoke, may also lay fire?

Rhodes himself felt the need to tweet recently that his

reasons for leaving were nothing to do with the EVPs or Punk but purely 'personal'. The fact that he felt the need to address this publicly illustrates that others have put two and two together. It should also be noted that several 'unnamed sources', who claim to be close to the Rhodes situation, have implied that his tweet was only half correct. Allegedly, the half that was true is that his leaving had nothing to do with CM Punk. Make of that what you will.

After everything that had gone down between them, few people at the time of their physical altercation blamed 'The Hitman' for what happened – despite most reports alleging him to be the aggressor. What's more, fans certainly didn't turn on him in mass because of it either. Yes, the world is a different place twenty-five years later but, just how different is it really? At least in the world of wrestling, things appear to be surprisingly similar. What has changed seemingly is fan acceptance of a real-life, physical confrontations. It's an odd contradiction in terms, when one considers that many of those same fans often desire increasing levels of physicality take place inside the ropes, with every passing year. I'd wager that most fans have cheered on certain wrestlers hitting their opponents way harder than any blow swung during 'brawl out' - irrespective of if said opponent had agreed to be hit that hard or not. We can also assume that those same fans listen intently to shoot interviews or cheer for promos or angles when the lines are blurred, such as MJF has done recently.

Perhaps with the word hypocrite being so freely banded around in situations like this, it could be wise for us all to look at ourselves and see what areas we too might be guilty of such a thing. Being quick to judge but slow to critically analyse appears to be what powers much of the internet in 2022, particularly in pro wrestling. If history has taught us one thing, it's that with each passing year, what was once the agreed narrative, slowly erodes to reveal cracks. Sometimes these cracks are so big that we decide that an entire nation or generation was 'on the wrong side of history'.

Yes, we can wash our hands of CM Punk, assuming that the current narrative is the real one. Yes, we can look upon his attitude as being incompatible with whatever the current trend tells us is the correct one. And yes, we can allow ourselves to watch him be cast aside because in the present climate, victims simply don't look or talk like him. Yet, watching many of the same fans who once cheered on his podcast with Colt Cabana or his arrival in AEW, now hoping that he goes back to WWE (who themselves are suddenly worth cheering again) could just be some of the biggest hypocrisy of all.

RULE OF ENGAGEMENT #14: CHANGE STRATEGY IF YOU'RE LOSING TERRITORY

As AEW licked its wounds after the 'Brawl Out' fiasco and tried to start afresh in 2023, the company faced a series of significant challenges that threatened its position in the wrestling industry. As well as the talent management problems raised by that incident, the story of 2022 had also been one of commercial struggles, creative criticism, and a shrinking market share relative to WWE.

As a business, AEW had been grappling with fluctuating success. While the company had made significant strides in pay-per-view sales and TV ratings in its early years, there was some evidence that its progress might now be stalling. Merchandise sales also reportedly plateaued and images started to circulate on social media of arenas with large sections of empty seats. Creatively, AEW faced criticism over its booking decisions and storyline coherence. Some story arcs, such as the extended feud between Chris Jericho and MJF, were perceived as overly drawn out, diminishing fan interest. Moreover, the company's approach to integrating new signings into its existing roster was often seen as haphazard, lacking clear direction or impactful storytelling.

This all happened just as WWE, now being driven

forwards by Triple H, was becoming more exciting than it had been in a long while. This was evident in key demographic data, where AEW's stronghold among younger viewers began to erode, a concerning trend for a promotion that prided itself on appealing to a newer generation of wrestling fans. An overhaul of AEW's tactics was urgently needed, but could Tony Khan really deliver the change in direction that was evidently needed?

CHAPTER 4
THE BIG PIVOT
ISSUE 47, FEBRUARY 2023

H G MCLAREN

AFTER THE MOST *difficult year in All Elite Wrestling's short history, H G McLaren looks at what lessons Tony Khan can learn from five of the worst calamities of the past twelve months, in order to avoid his new business becoming just another statistic.*

It's hard to argue that 2022 was nothing less than AEW's most challenging year to date. From the outside looking in, some may refer to it as close to catastrophic. Indeed, in this article alone, we will dissect five individual occurrences which, had they happened in isolation, would be cause for serious concern to any company. The fact that all five of them transpired within the same twelve-month period could be easily described as disastrous. With words like 'disastrous', 'catastrophic', or 'serious concern' already being used just a mere four sentences in, you could be mistaken into thinking that this is going to be a 'doom and gloom' article about AEW's less than rosy future. In reality, what follows is intended to be the complete opposite. Before we reach that point however, it will be beneficial to take a short detour.

There have always been many giant misconceptions about business. In fact, such misconceptions are not exclusively held only by those on the outsides, devoid of any practical business experience or knowledge – far from it. Such misconceptions are also rife amongst those actually running businesses themselves. So much so in fact, that they often kill a business from the inside before it's even really started. According to the U.S Bureau of Labour Statistics, one in five businesses fail within the first year of trading. Of the four that remain, two of them will be dead within the next five years. In short, statistically speaking, a business that remains solvent and operational after five years has done very well. These stats are more relevant to AEW, and at this exact time, than some readers may first realise.

All Elite Wrestling was founded in January 2019. As the article that you are currently reading gets released in January 2023, the next twelve months will determine if the company becomes one that is here to stay or, alternatively, simply another victim in the aforementioned statistics of business failure. At this point, it would be fair to argue that comparing a business which was founded by the son of a billionaire to a small, self-funded start-up, created in someone's garage makes little sense. After all, according to the same statistics, eighty two percent of businesses fail due to outstanding debts and cash flow problems – something unlikely to happen with Tony Khan. Yet, to focus on this alone, is to miss the far bigger picture. Companies running out of money isn't really the cause of most businesses failing, but rather, the effect.

BUSINESS AS USUAL

It might be odd to consider now, but at certain points in the creation of their companies, the world's two richest men, Jeff Bezos and Elon Musk, both ran out of money when building the businesses that would ultimately build their fortunes. In fact, at one point Bezos required (and received) a cash injection into Amazon of a staggering $680 million dollars, as without it, the company would surely die. What made this mammoth investment even more staggering was that the company wasn't even turning a profit at the point. It was a similar story with Elon Musk and SpaceX, whose first three rocket launches failed in spectacular fashion. If the fourth had failed, the company would have run out of money and quickly died. Luckily for Musk, in his own words, the 'fourth time was a charm', the rocket launched successfully, enormous NASA contracts ensured, and the rest is history.

In both instances, it proves that a lack of funds often only kills a company if the core business itself isn't investable or worthy of a loan. In other words, a sustainable business will always have options available to it, even if it is currently unprofitable. An unsustainable one on the other hand, can only last as long as the money that it currently has. Therefore, to clarify an earlier premise, running out of money is an 'effect' of a business's failure and not the 'cause'. So, what then, really makes the difference between a business that succeeds and one that fails? Furthermore, are there lessons that AEW and we as fans can learn from them?

To answer the second question first, yes, there are absolutely lessons that we and Tony Khan can gleam from them and this article intends to focus in on several of them in granular detail. Before that, however, lets address the first question; what really makes the difference between a business that succeeds and one that fails? It's true that the answer can vary wildly, especially as it relates to those fortunate few who managed to capture lighting in a bottle, almost from its inception such as Facebook. Yet for the majority, there are certainly some hard and fast rules that can be applied across the board. Indeed, misunderstanding the most important of these rules is the reason that, despite its seemingly unstoppable decade plus long rise, Mark Zuckerberg has seen his company's share price drop by some seventy percent in recent times. If the

tion into Amazon of a staggering $680 million dollars, as without it, the company would surely die. What made this mammoth investment even more staggering was that the company wasn't even turning a profit at the point. It was a similar story with Elon Musk and SpaceX, whose first three rocket launches failed in spectacular fashion. If the fourth had failed, the company would have run out of money and quickly died. Luckily for Musk, in his own words, the 'fourth time was a charm', the rocket launched successfully, enormous NASA contracts ensured, and the rest is history.

In both instances, it proves that a lack of funds often only kills a company if the core business itself isn't investable or worthy of a loan. In other words, a sustainable business will always have options available to it, even if it is currently unprofitable. An unsustainable one on the other hand, can only last as long as the money that it currently has. Therefore, to clarify an earlier premise, running out of money is an 'effect' of a business's failure and not the 'cause'. So, what then, really makes the difference between a business that succeeds and one that fails? Furthermore, are there lessons that AEW and we as fans can learn from them?

To answer the second question first, yes, there are absolutely lessons that we and Tony Khan can gleam from them and this article intends to focus in on several of them in granular detail. Before that, however, lets address the first question; what really makes the difference between a business that succeeds and one that fails? It's true that the answer can vary wildly, especially as it relates to those fortunate few who managed to capture lighting in a bottle, almost from its inception such as Facebook. Yet for the majority, there are certainly some hard and fast rules that can be applied across the board. Indeed, misunderstanding the most important of these rules is the reason that, despite its seemingly unstoppable decade plus long rise, Mark Zuckerberg has seen his company's share price drop by some seventy percent in recent times. If the lesson is good enough for Facebook – or sorry, Meta – then it's certainly good enough for wrestling's only real potential competitor to the WWE.

The lesson is simple; there are two businesses to every business owner. The one that they think they are building and the one which they actually have. At the start, a business has grand plans, big ideas and are awash with outside influences, suggesting one potential route or another. It's often these factors that power a start-up to be created. Additionally, it's been proven that being somewhat delusional is often a much-needed component in starting a business. After all, one look at our statistic from earlier should be enough for any sane person to run straight to the nearest employer and beg for a cosy job, along with the fixed salary, holiday time and sweet benefits that come with it. Not so with entrepreneurs. They look at the eighty percent failure rate, laugh in its face and do it anyway! Yet, while a bit of healthy delusion might be useful in overcoming the fear of failure when creating a company, it's often an atrocious trait for actually running and operating a successful business over the long haul. This is particularly true when a founder's earlier plans, misconceptions or inexperience come face to face with the harsh realities of the commercial world. Once the business that they thought they were building begins to fall apart, a delusional owner will ignore the warning signs and keep on pushing against the tide. A sage one on the other hand, will read those same signs and make the necessary adjustments to their operation – even if that means changing course entirely. In the start-up world, this is called a 'pivot'.

Those founders that grasp this early enough and pivot accordingly are quickly introduced to their second business – the one that they are actually making; no matter how far removed it might be from that which they had prior. Sometimes this pivot is forced by a radical change in technology, such as how the invention of the iPhone spawned a wave of huge app-based businesses. Occasionally, the pivot comes as the result of a founder believing that they've glimpsed the future and want to prepare for it early – much is the case with the aforementioned Facebook and their attempt to fully own the impending Metaverse. Yet, on occasion, the need for a pivot comes from a continued onslaught of serious issues. All of which force a business owner to accept that there is a fundamental problem which needs remedying imminently. After the 2022 that they've just endured, few companies more aptly fit into this category than All Elite Wrestling.

What follows are five of the biggest issues that AEW faced in the last year. Crucially, each comes with the hugely important lessons that Tony Khan can learn from them, allowing his promotion to pivot and grow, as it approaches its fifth year. The year in which the statistics claim that the company's chance of success is 50/50.

CODY RHODES LEAVES AEW — FOR WWE

Not so long ago, it was unthinkable that Cody Rhodes, one of the original founders of AEW and the loudest voice against the WWE, would leave the promotion he'd helped to create – least of all, to go back with the company that he'd been so vocally opposed to. Yet, with 2022 being a year of almost unprecedented twists and turns in the world of pro wrestling – the 'unthinkable' wasn't even the biggest news story of the year. What it was, however, was the first real sign that behind the welcoming and excitable exterior of All Elite Wrestling, all wasn't exactly as well as it might first appear.

Many theories circulated about Cody's departure. One in particular centred around alleged issues between he and his fellow EVP's – a story which would gain more traction later, with events that were yet to transpire. As it's likely that

Rhodes signed some form of non-disparagement agreement with his former employer before exiting the company, the truth of what really caused him to leave will likely remain unknown for some time – if not forever. Irrespective of that, this article is not about why the issues that AEW faced in 2022 happened, but rather, what they can learn from them going forwards. In that regard, Rhodes' departure, if treated correctly, could be a net positive.

It's clear that from day one, nobody in AEW management were more public in their war time stance towards the WWE than Rhodes. In fact, even some hardcore AEW supporters saw his 'sledgehammering' of a Triple H style throne at the promotion's inaugural Double or Nothing event in 2019, as a needlessly tacky shot against the industry leader. Considering where he now works, even Rhodes himself may wince a little when he remembers doing it. For those watching on with a more balanced perspective, this act appeared to detract from what AEW's real mission should be – entertaining wrestling fans with good content, not using valuable airtime for personal grudges or needless pot shots. Something that WWE had previously often done and were rightly criticised for. While it was true that many fans were desperate for a new wrestling war to begin, it was somewhat delusional (that word again) for AEW to presume that they were anything close to 'war ready', particularly against a foe so established and large, especially so soon after their official launch. At best, it was an unneeded distraction for AEW management and supporters a like. At worst, it was AEW being tone deaf to reality and somewhat petulant.

As the skit was not so covertly symbolic, it acted as a warning shot to the WWE – AEW is coming for you. AEW didn't see itself as the underdog, but rather a true competitor to the McMahon empire. This would only serve to bite AEW in the backside in the months and years which followed, where Tony Khan and others would cry foul of WWE and the various tactics that they were using against the new company. How could the underdog complain about WWE attacking them and receive any real sympathy, when AEW themselves had fired such a public shot and so early on? Also, if wrestling has taught us one thing, it's that pissing off Triple H is never a good idea. More on that later.

Several believe that this throne incident would never have happened if Tony Khan had full control of the creative output at the time, as he would later gain. In avoiding this skit, AEW's back and forth battle with WWE would have likely been less prominent, at least so early on, allowing Khan and co to be proactive in creating a great company instead of reactively focusing on how to get one over on WWE. In short, Khan and AEW by default may have inadvertently inherited a war from Cody that they didn't really want or need – at least so soon. It would be a war that altered the shape of AEW and potentially many of their steps which followed. It was also a war that, as time would tell, even Rhodes himself was not that committed to fighting for.

THE BRAWL OUT AFTER ALL OUT

The wrestling news cycle has exhausted the backstage fall out from 2022's 'All Out' event and thus, little more needs adding here. What is of note though, is the side which Tony Khan decided to back – his original EVP's. While it is largely agreed that the arrival of CM Punk to AEW was the highlight of the company thus far from both a publicity and revenue perspective, it's also clear that the whole episode wasn't without its issues – even prior to 'Brawl Out'. Punk appeared injury prone; a real issue in a promotion centred largely around athletic or physically intense performances. Then there were the problems around power and influence in AEW; who has it and who is losing it? These problems no doubt had some baring over Cody Rhodes' decision to leave. With a marquee name as large as Punk joining the mix, you can only imagine the shifting company dynamics that such an arrival would cause behind the scenes – especially post Cody's exit and the power vacuum that it created.

Although there is certainly a view by some that Khan made the wrong decision in siding with Kenny Omega and The Young Bucks over his highest grossing, box office attraction, one thing has to be said; he at least made a choice and stuck to it. More so, he made an extremely tough decision and one that few others would have had the conviction or courage to make, irrespective of if it was the correct one or not. In so doing, Khan made a clear line in the sand as it relates to where the true power in AEW lays… with him and him alone.

After all, nobody was made to look worse or more undermined from the All Out press conference than Tony Khan himself – even though that was likely not Punk's intention. By being forced to sit there while his top star buried the promotion, some of its talent and several members of key management, Khan was made to look like a man not in control of his own company. By making the subsequent decision that he made after the backstage altercation, Khan firmly established that he is not afraid to send talent packing, no matter how big a star they might be. In doing so, he set a clear precedent for others to be wary of in the future. Thus, potentially avoiding many of the pitfalls that both WCW and TNA encountered, when letting their top talent call the shots, often at the expense of the wider business as a whole.

THE ARIEL HELWANI INTERVIEW

On October 6th, one month after the events of 'Brawl Out', distinguished MMA journalist, Ariel Helwani released a YouTube interview that he'd just conducted with Tony Khan. Being charitable, the interview would be best described as uncomfortable. Being not so kind, many called it a car crash. In fact, Helwani himself publicly referred to it "one of the most frustrating and not so fun interviews of my career". Pretty harsh words, right?

What made this interview so 'frustrating' then? In short, because Khan refused to be used as a sound bite machine, providing private information about the 'fall out from brawl out' which would no doubt only help feed even more 'AEW is doomed' news headlines. Annoyingly for Khan, those headlines were instead changed to 'Tony Khan in car crash interview', likely getting even more traction, particularly once Helwani himself added to the negative sentiment. However, the position that Khan took was not only the correct one, but also, potentially the start of a much more important change in direction for AEW's true founding father.

It's been said prior, even in this magazine, that Khan must take some blame for CM Punk's All Out media scrum rant. After all, Khan's primarily the person who'd created the 'gloves off', shoot interview style, press conference format that takes place after each of AEW's main shows. It's a format borrowed largely from the UFC and Dana White – someone who's previously had his own major issues with Helwani in the past. By creating such a platform, where Khan himself would, on occasion, share his own wild theories, frustrations and grievances, why then, wouldn't Punk feel that he was entitled do the same? After all, who is the master of the pipe bomb, no less? This, coupled with Khan's seeming desire to be public friends with everyone and the smiling face of All

Elite Wrestling, meant that something was destined to come undone someday. Especially in the world's current climate.

For the first time ever in history, and much as was covered with the likes of Bezos, Musk and Zuckerberg, the world now has a super class of billionaires. In a period where much of the planet faces real socio-economic issues, more scrutiny than ever is being placed on whether such western oligarchs are actually benefiting our society or hurting it. After all, it's hard to defend Amazon's mistreatment of its warehouse workers or delivery staff, when the money that their labour has earned affords Bezos the privilege of sending himself up into space, and wearing a cowboy hat no less! No matter how smiley his presentation in AEW, Tony Khan comes from this same billionaire class. His audience on the other hand, fall firmly on the other side. To pretend that a level of jealously towards Khan doesn't already exist and won't continue to increase with each passing month, is naive. Afterall, what fans doesn't wish that they had a rich enough father to buy them a wrestling company as a toy?

When factoring all of this into the larger picture, it appears clear that the AEW front facing Tony Khan of old may need to rethink his public image, over exposure and a tendency to both gloat and play the victim in equal measure. The interview with Ariel Helwani may have been the crucial catalyst for this change. After all, with Helwani's links to WWE and some of their top-level people so apparent, not to mention the interview that he conducted with MJF which created all the friction between he and AEW, why would Khan not assume that he could have been walking into an ambush of sorts? Especially given the proximity of the interview in relation to 'brawl out' and all of the media attention that came with it? If this 'car crash' teaches Khan that saying less can often mean more, to be unafraid of not being everyone's friend, and ultimately, reduces his desire to be so visible at every opportunity, then it could become an extremely valuable turning point for the promotion.

ROH'S TV DEAL — OR LACK OF IT

When Tony Khan bought Ring of Honor, insiders speculated just how much he paid for it. The number ranged somewhere from between ten and forty million dollars, depending on who you asked. Even the low end of that spectrum was a whopping four times the $2.5M that Vince McMahon had paid for WCW! Yet, unlike the 'how' of the ROH deal, very few column inches were put into the 'why' of it. Why did Khan make this purchase? And most importantly, 'what', would he do with the brand now? Onlookers speculated over a grand plan, which would soon be revealed. The reality that they were later to receive from the ROH acquisition would be far less spectacular.

After months of talk about a potential ROH TV deal, as of early January 2023, no such deal is happening. In fact, after an initially positive start, the ROH purchase appears to have become more of a distraction than a net positive for Tony Khan and All Elite Wrestling as a whole. By splitting Khan's creative focus over two brands, whilst massively increasing his already bloated talent roster, outside of any tape library benefits, it's hard to see what Khan gained from the deal. Surely that money could have been spent on further growing AEW's global footprint or hiring more talented management executives from larger media companies? Executives who could have aided in reducing some of Khan's countless responsibilities – leaving him more time to focus on his core strengths.

With all of this in mind, it has to be pondered if Khan brought ROH, simply because he wanted to beat the WWE in owning the archive? Yes, he and many of his roster have a sentimental attachment to ROH - that's understandable. However, once you remove sentiment from the deal, it's hard to see the acquisition as anything more than an overly expensive, impulse purchase, all with very little value to AEW - outside of bragging rights. What's worse, the distraction of Khan by ROH, as it does any business owner, comes at a cost to AEW too. Either Khan's time is split and thus AEW suffers from the loss of his attention. Or he replaces himself with other people and those people cost money too. Oh, and that's not to mention the day to day running costs of having a second brand. Either way, whatever Khan paid Sinclair Broadcasting is only the beginning of the real-world expenditure that comes with this deal.

But all is not lost. Learning this lesson now might have been a pricey one but entering into the company's fifth year, it's statistical make or break, at least will give Khan pause for thought when the next down and out wrestling brand comes knocking at his door. With the global economy in the shape that it currently is, it's likely that another knock or two will arrive before 2023 is out.

WILLIAM REGAL JOINING AEW — AND THEN LEAVING SUDDENLY

When William Regal was let go by WWE, speculated to be part of Vince McMahon's purge of Triple H's inner circle as part of the punishment for NXT losing its ratings war against AEW Dynamite, most predicted what would happen next. After all, with Regal being one of the most respected veterans and mentors of talent ever to work behind the WWE's iron curtain, why wouldn't Tony Khan sign him? Furthermore, once being so close to the seat of power in his biggest rival, the signing of Regal could be lauded as a major coup for Khan and AEW. Khan however overlooked one obvious truth; money can't buy loyalty.

Khan might have viewed the hiring of Regal as a satisfying 'screw you' to Triple H, sure. Yet it was a mistake for him to believe that a short-term payday would overturn the long-term trust, loyalty and friendship that had been built between the former 'Man's Man' and 'The Game', over their near three-decade long relationship. While surrounding yourself with an adversary's old inner circle appears wise on paper, in practice, the realities are often very different – especially if that adversary is not yet dead! Despite a huge push with, first 'The Blackpool Combat Club' and later, alongside MJF in arguably AEW's most intriguing storyline, Regal would leave shortly after Vince McMahon 'walked away' from WWE and Triple reclaimed his previous power and then some. Not only did AEW receive a black eye both creatively and reputationally in the process, with another high-level defection, but there was worse. Khan had now also provided an inside look at how AEW was being run during its most chaotic period, and to a man that was primed to go right back to the one person Khan didn't want to know any of it – Triple H.

Knowing who to trust and who not, is a vital part of any business. Building an inner circle of trusted advisors and confidants can be painstaking, if not heart-breaking; especially in the often-unscrupulous world of pro wrestling. While surrounding yourself with the men who were once your enemies can be alluring, especially with the short-term sense of victory that it can provide, the pitfalls of this approach are frequently high. Afterall, very few can be on the losing side of a battle without secretly having their own axe to grind against the winning party. Those who engage in this slippery slope need to be aware that if such an axe exists, it could end up directly between your shoulder blades, if you're not paying close attention.

None of this is to say that Regal's intentions were negative. In fact, after having a front row seat during AEW's most turbulent year ever, returning to the relative safety of WWE, now being run by somebody that he's been friends with for over thirty years, is a very understandable move. This is not about Regal. It's about Tony Khan. If this scenario should have taught him anything, it's the following; while my enemy's enemy may be my friend, my enemy's recently released right-hand man, isn't always my instant ally. Hopefully learning this lesson so publicly will inform similar choices that Khan might consider in 2023. After all, if the previous year has taught us anything, it's that WWE's current inner circle can change in an instant and the fall out can often leave a plethora of hungry mouths, all looking for someone new to feed them. Hell, who's to say that the next twelve months won't be without the return of Vince McMahon and even more of the same?

TURNING POINT?

Much like Dixie Carter before Khan, being quick to replicate everything that WWE once did, isn't always the smartest move for a new promotion. While some businesses thrive from simply duplicating the market leaders approach but offering a slightly different alternative, such as Pepsi to Coke or Burger King to McDonalds, that can also be a risky strategy. This is especially true in the creative sector, which wrestling certainly falls into, and when a company has spent so much time bashing the business practices of the industry leader in the first place. After all, it's problematic to claim how evil WWE's operations truly are to all who will listen, when at every given opportunity you borrow directly from their handbook. Yes, all businesses can and should learn from their rivals but to attempt such a 'cut and paste' approach to your own inner workings is lazy, uninspired and ultimately, leads to most becoming nothing more than a watered down version of the very business that they've told their customers is 'the enemy'. Too many in wrestling have tried this approach previously and failed. The ones who succeeded, albeit momentarily, such as ECW, TNA and WCW, attempted to do and be something radically different from what the WWE was offering.

In fact, this concept isn't a new one, even to AEW. When the company launched, it promised a multitude of things that would offer a true alternative to the WWE. Anyone else remember it's heavily touted but barely delivered, sports style rankings system? Yet, almost from the moment that Cody Rhodes' sledgehammer touched down, followed by a frankly embarrassing pyro throne detonation, AEW moved in a different direction. What followed were several years of Tony Khan focusing on the business that he thought he was building. In 2022, so many elements of that imagined business fell apart, that it's inconceivable for anybody in Khan's position not to be considering a serious change of direction. If he can use the lessons of 2022 to pivot into the company that he is actually building, shifting his focus from WWE and the reactive tendencies that have spawned from it, 2023 could well become the year that AEW discovers the company that it truly is. If it doesn't, you can be sure that the picture of Khan on Triple H's metaphorical dartboard will have a continued barrage of projectiles piercing it in the year to come. There are only so many more of those darts that All Elite Wrestling can take before the brand goes down in history as just another business that proves the failure statistics correct. As wrestling fans, we should all be hoping that such a sad end to such an initially encouraging brand, doesn't happen.

RULE OF ENGAGEMENT #15: ENSURE YOUR ARMY HAS THE DEEPEST WAR CHEST

In early 2023, as WWE geared up for crucial TV rights negotiations, the company faced a significant upheaval at the board level, marked by the unexpected return of its former chairman. Vince McMahon's dramatic comeback was a strategic manoeuvre that caught many within and outside the company by surprise. After stepping down in the summer of 2022 amid various controversies, McMahon forced his way back onto the board by leveraging his majority voting power. He effectively ousted three existing board members - JoEllen Lyons Dillon, Jeffrey R. Speed, and Alan M. Wexler - and reinstated himself, along with two of his allies, Michelle Wilson and George Barrios, both former WWE executives.

McMahon justified his re-entry under the guise of exploring "strategic alternatives" for WWE, including a potential sale. This move was deemed critical by McMahon, especially considering the impending renegotiation of television rights for WWE's flagship shows, Monday Night RAW and Friday Night SmackDown. McMahon apparently believed that his presence and direct involvement would maximise the value and outcome of these negotiations - although many believed he also wanted to secure a deal that would allow him to make his return to the helm a permanent one.

McMahon's return sparked a mixture of reactions. While some stakeholders viewed his experience and business acumen as assets in high-stakes negotiations, others expressed concern over the potential impact on the company's direction and public image. McMahon's previous departure had paved the way for a creative overhaul under Paul 'Triple H' Levesque, which had been positively received by fans and critics. There were fears that McMahon's involvement could derail this progress and lead to a shift back to the old ways of operating. But on the surface at least, McMahon's reasoning was sound - after all, TV rights fees had long since become the main source of the company's wealth, ensuring that - contrary to what many casual observers may have assumed - WWE had never been more profitable than it was at this moment.

CHAPTER 5
THEY'VE NEVER HAD IT SO GOOD

ISSUE 48, APRIL 2023
DAVE BRADSHAW

DOESN'T *it seem odd that WWE is more profitable than ever despite its ratings and live attendance being way below what they were in the Attitude Era? Dave Bradshaw was feeling puzzled, so he decided to try and crunch the numbers...*

I'll be honest: for several years now whenever WWE release their latest financial reports I have always felt quietly puzzled but didn't want to say anything in case I was the only person on Twitter too stupid to understand what was going on. Because it is publicly traded, the company is required under US law to report both quarterly and annually on its operations, including financial statements, and these reports are made available to the general public in order to provide transparency for potential investors. Almost without fail, every one of these reports issued by the McMahon business empire seems to trumpet record-breaking performance - and I didn't get it.

The most recent example is the full year report for 2022, which was delivered at the start of February. It showed that the company had $1.29 billion revenue over the course of the year, and after their various running costs were deducted they still made a profit of $193.3 million. Both the revenue and profit numbers were all-time records for WWE, and it was the fourth year in a row that they had set a new all-time high. Even if you adjust for inflation, the most financially successful years in the Attitude Era (2000 and 2001) did less than half as well. The most financially successful year of the Hulkamania era was 1990, and that was only about a quarter as lucrative as 2022.

That all just seemed totally mind-boggling. After all, as often as we hear about the company's financial success we also see reports of its popularity being on the wane: graphs showing TV ratings trending downwards for a number of years, photos on social media of half-empty arenas for TV tapings, Google searches for WWE and its top stars in steady decline. Anecdotally we feel it too: those of us old enough to remember the era of Stone Cold and The Rock remember how much mainstream buzz there was around them, how WWE was legitimately popular among young people. Admittedly, anyone who was a teenager in those days is now rapidly approaching middle age and probably doesn't have their finger on the pulse of what today's kids think is cool, but it doesn't take an expert in youth culture to see that the likes of Roman Reigns and Becky Lynch - despite their best efforts - don't have quite the same place in the zeitgeist as some of their predecessors. Still, to be totally sure that I wasn't just becoming one of those old people who prattles on about how much better things were in my day, I decided it was time to gather some data.

The first place I looked was at the TV ratings, where all these reports of a decline are accurate: at around the turn of the century when Austin was battling McMahon and everyone was smelling what The Rock was cooking, Raw regularly did over 6.0 in the US ratings and occasionally even hit 7.0 (meaning that 7% of households were watching it, estimated to be about 9 million people), despite being up against competition from WCW Nitro. Smackdown wasn't far behind it, with a rating that was often around 5.0 on Thursday nights. But during the two decades since that time those numbers have steadily dropped off, and nowadays both Raw and Smackdown perform weekly at about the 2.0 range, meaning that fewer than 2 million people are watching.

There are a few important caveats to that trend, however. For one thing, it is hard to compare viewing figures directly with those from 20 or more years ago - this is because back then the only way for most people to watch a show at a time other than when it actually broadcast was to record it on a VHS, whereas nowadays people routinely watch programmes on demand after they have aired, making the live figures less important than they once were. For another thing, in recent years TV networks have paid far less attention to overall ratings and have been more concerned with particular demographics - specifically with the 18-49 age group, who are believed to be the most attractive to advertisers. And thirdly, there is now more competition than ever for viewers' attention - including from streaming services like Netflix - meaning that many long-running shows have seen decreases in their ratings over time. For all of these reasons it is worth remembering that direct comparisons with the past are tricky, but even taking all of that into account there is little doubt that WWE's ratings have trended downwards across the board.

Next I looked into live show attendance. Given that AEW has recently announced plans to start running house shows in addition to its TV tapings, it was interesting to first see how many of these untelevised events WWE has scheduled each year. In short, the basic trend for the number of shows WWE produces per year has increased since the Attitude Era, when it sometimes ran as few as 100. That figure basically doubled from 2002 when the company first split Raw and Smackdown into separate rosters who would tour independently of each other, thus allowing shows to run in two different cities on the same evening. The company therefore held around 200 house shows per year from 2002 until the mid-2010s, when the output was ratcheted up further again (partly thanks to NXT touring as a third brand), and by the end of the decade the number was around 400 per year. Obviously that number turned to zero during the pandemic, and it remains to be seen if it will return to previous levels over the long term.

Meanwhile, attendance at all of those events is down on what it was during the glory days of the late 90s when the average number of people in the arena for a WWE event was close to 11,000 (meaning that in many cases they were sold out or not far off). By 2004 the average attendance had been cut in half to somewhere around 5500 - but since then, despite all those horror stories about empty arenas, the average attendance has stayed pretty much the same year on year. And of course, in a few important areas the live gates are better than ever: in particular at Wrestlemania, which is now always held in a large stadium and has recently expanded to being held over two nights. Ticket prices at the Showcase of the Immortals are way up on what they were too: for example, in 2008 a ticket to watch Ric Flair retire at the Citrus Bowl cost about $90, whereas getting into the same venue nine years later to see the Hardy Boyz return to WWE would have set you back an average of over $220. This steady rise in prices contributed to last year's Mania in Dallas bringing in a record $18 million over two nights, and the 2023 edition in Los Angeles is set to do better still.

One more area I decided to explore is how the company's fortunes have varied in terms of its pay-per-views, or "premium live events" as the kids are calling them. This is the hardest thing of all to analyse, for the simple reason that WWE essentially abandoned the pay-per-view business when it launched the WWE Network in 2014 so we cannot simply compare pay-per-view buys in 2023 to those of the Attitude Era. However, we can look at how things were trending up to

2014. In the four Attitude Era years of 1998 to 2001 the company's pay-per-views achieved an average of 451,000 buys in North America. Between 2010 and 2013, the four years immediately before the launch of the Network, they were averaging 182,000 buys. Aside from Wrestlemania, which was still doing huge numbers (often over a million buys), this is another part of the business that had clearly declined.

THE RIGHTS BONANZA

Hopefully all of these statistics haven't made your head explode - but just to be on the safe side, let's recap: whether you look at TV ratings, live event attendance or pay-per-view numbers, it is clear that modern-day WWE is less popular with the public than it was at the height of the Attitude Era. In that case, how on Earth is the company achieving record amounts of revenue and profit every year? The answer, perhaps surprisingly, is that WWE's financial success is less dependent than ever on taking money directly from wrestling fans. Instead, its biggest sources of income by far are its various TV rights deals around the world, and its multi-year deal to host live events in Saudi Arabia. Or, to put all of that in corporate jargon, the company relies far less on Business To Consumers (B2C) and far more on Business To Business (B2B). As recently as 2008, about 78% of WWE's revenue came from B2C - in other words, from selling things directly to the public - whether that be live event tickets, pay-per-views, DVD sales or other merchandise. Only 22% of its income was from B2B sources such as selling the rights to broadcast its TV shows. Nowadays almost the exact opposite is true: 78% of the company's revenue is B2B, and that part of the business has absolutely exploded in value. But why?

Well, first let's consider the Saudi Arabia deal. In 2017, WWE agreed a 10-year deal to host two events per year in the country for about $50 million per show, or $1 billion over the course of a decade. To put that into perspective, the combined ticket revenue from every Wrestlemania ever is less than $250 million (i.e. a quarter of a billion dollars). The Saudi government has been investing huge sums into bringing popular sporting events into the country, which has been hugely controversial for reasons that you probably already know (in fact we covered the subject in detail in issue 35) - but regardless of the ethics, make no mistake about the fact that this is an absolute monster of a deal for WWE.

Still, even the Saudi deal pales in comparison to how much WWE now receives in TV rights fees. There was a time back in the 1980s and early 1990s when the company actually paid the TV networks to broadcast its content, with the logic being that having the product on national TV served as a great infomercial to drive the sale of pay-per-views and live event tickets. By the Attitude Era that had changed and WWE was being paid for its content, but on nothing like the scale of the fees it receives today. In 2001 WWE received a combined total of about $44 million per year (or $850,000 per week) for the US broadcast rights to Raw and Smackdown. By 2010 that figure was around $77 million per year, and a new five-year deal starting in 2014 was worth $131 million per year. Then in 2018 the company appointed agent (and future WWE CEO) Nick Khan to lead its negotiations for the next five-year period, and managed to secure deals with USA Network for Raw and with FOX for Smackdown, the combined total of which was a whopping $470 million per year. That's $9 million every week that the company now receives for Raw and Smackdown in the US - more than 10 times what it got in 2001. Even adjusting for inflation, WWE's TV rights fees are worth at least six times as much now as they were two decades ago.

How can it be even remotely possible that TV networks in 2023 want to pay so much more than they did in 2001 for a product that is less popular with audiences now than it was then? One word: advertising. As you probably know, commercial television networks make much of their income from companies paying to show ads during their programmes. Unfortunately for them, the past few years have seen most households obtain the technology to record their favourite TV shows on a DVR and watch them back at a convenient time, fast forwarding through the ad breaks. This means that fewer people watch the ads, so the brands are not willing to pay as much. However, there are a few types of programming that are considered to be "DVR-proof" - in other words, people want to watch certain broadcasts live as they happen rather than watching them later on demand, so they will sit through the ad breaks too. The main type of content that falls into this category is live sporting events, because viewers want to watch the action as it happens rather than hours later when they have probably already learned what the final score was.

While wrestling might not quite be a live sporting event, it seems that audiences treat it that way: the percentage of viewers who watch Raw live rather than on demand is much higher than most non-sports programming, presumably because viewers still want to avoid spoilers in the same way that they would with an NFL game. While the number of people watching Raw each week might be way down on what it was a few years ago, it still attracts more live viewers than the vast majority of non-sports programming. Brands are prepared to pay big money to advertise during broadcasts with this kind of upside, and in turn TV networks are prepared to pay enormous fees to secure the rights to such content. In fact, the most popular American sports have done even better than WWE's $470 million per year: the NFL gets an unfathomable $10.2 billion per year in rights fees under its most recent deal, while the NBA nets $2.6 billion and Major League Baseball gets around $1.75 billion. Of course, that's just for rights to show the sports in the US market - the amounts are even more astronomical if you take into account the rest of the world. In WWE's case these international deals include one worth around $50 million per year in India, a reported $20 million per year in the UK, and similar multimillion dollar agreements in other markets.

THE BUBBLE MAY NOT BURST

So, the short answer to the question of why WWE is more lucrative now than ever before despite its waning popularity is simple - it's because we are living through a genuinely remarkable boom period in TV rights fees. Of course, that begs another question: will that bubble eventually burst? If so then WWE could potentially find itself much more dependent than it is now on the B2C activities that used to comprise the majority of its revenue; if its fanbase continues to shrink then this could leave the company in a much more precarious position than it is today. That sounds scary, but the good news for WWE is that there's no sign of things changing any time soon. On the contrary, "DVR-proof" programmes are now seen as so important that it isn't just traditional TV networks who are bidding for them - the likes of Amazon, Netflix, Disney and Apple are all showing increased interest in joining the bidding war when it comes time to renew the rights deals for major sports. WWE's deal with Peacock is one of the first major 'sports' content grabs by an online subscription platform, but it certainly won't be the last.

This is the backdrop against which WWE is preparing to negotiate its next TV rights deal for the US market. The current bumper deal brokered by Nick Khan started in 2019 and expires in 2024, so discussions about the next deal are expected to begin in the very near future. In Raw's case the smart money is probably on a new and improved deal being agreed with the USA Network, which the show has called home for much of its 30-year existence. After all, USA is owned by NBCUniversal and Peacock is NBC's streaming service, so the connections to WWE run deep. Far less certain is the fate of Smackdown: according to some reports FOX has not been thrilled with the ratings it has been achieving on Friday nights, so it's entirely possible that they might decide not to bid for the next deal or might make a bid that is below WWE's valuation. On the other hand, at $4 million per week Smackdown is a relatively cheap way for FOX to fill two hours of prime time television every Friday night, and it generally performs well in the ratings compared to what the other major networks are offering in the same timeslot.

Nonetheless, it is far from implausible that Smackdown could leave FOX, either for another network or for a streaming service. There is reason to believe that WWE themselves might prefer to do a deal with a streaming service, or at least with a company like NBCUniversal that has an established streaming platform as well as traditional TV channels on which to make WWE programming available. While traditional TV remains the most popular way of consuming content, the market share of streaming services is increasing over time, especially with the 18 to 49 demographic that advertisers prize so highly. Peacock is a very good example of this: it had 9 million subscribers at the end of 2021, but had more than doubled this to 20 million by the end of 2022. That's why you might have heard WWE touting this year's Royal Rumble and Elimination Chamber as the "most-watched" editions of those events in history: so many people now have access to Peacock that setting new viewership records is almost inevitable. It therefore makes sense that WWE would want to work with a broadcast partner that has a substantial streaming business, so that there will be more eyes on the product. NBC and a few other suitors can provide such a platform - but not every network can.

Of course, there is one other big factor that might affect the upcoming rights negotiations. Unless you have spent the first part of 2023 living under a rock you will know that WWE has said that it is currently exploring "strategic alternatives" including a possible sale of the company. The timing of that announcement is deliberate, as some potential buyers might want to make their move before any future rights deal is agreed. For example, if someone like Disney Plus was considering whether to make a bid for the broadcast rights to Smackdown, they might decide that it made more sense to buy WWE as a whole rather than pay hundreds of millions of dollars to gain the TV rights for a limited number of years. Inevitably it's not just about the economic arithmetic though: there are other factors for any potential buyer to consider, such as whether they really want to become involved in the day-to-day workings of a business as quirky as pro wrestling, and whether the current 77-year-old owner of the company might insist that a condition of any sale is that he be allowed to remain in charge.

With all of this in mind there are a lot of unknowns for WWE as 2023 unfolds, but ultimately the company is clearly in an enviable position: it continues to ride the wave of a TV rights bonanza that has made it more profitable than at any time in its history. That has insulated it against the fact that it has been gradually fading in popularity among consumers since its heyday in the late 1990s. But even on that front there are reasons to be optimistic. WWE, and indeed the wrestling industry more generally, has shown a remarkable capacity through the decades for reinvention, and for eventually finding a way to push itself back into the mainstream of popular culture. If it can find a way to reignite the B2C part of the business at the same time as the B2B part continues to thrive then we may yet see a new golden age for the company that would dwarf even those heady days of the Attitude Era…

WAS LAUNCHING THE WWE NETWORK A GOOD OR BAD MOVE IN HINDSIGHT?

It used to all be very straightforward: WWE's big monthly shows were available via pay-per-view at a price of up to $60 each depending on the event, and their weekly programmes on cable TV attempted to persuade as many viewers as possible to cough up the cash for the next one of those events. That was always the business model, but by 2013 there was a feeling that too much money was being left on the table: Wrestlemania was typically getting around a million buys each year and the Royal Rumble might do half a million, but most other pay-per-views were only attracting around 200,000 customers - and some drew considerably less. Given that Raw was still reliably getting around 4 million weekly viewers at that time, it meant that only about one in every 20 Raw viewers was being convinced to buy the pay-per-view in most months. When you look at it that way, you can see why a change in approach didn't seem like the craziest of ideas - and so the WWE Network was born.

From early 2014 fans were invited to pay $9.99 per month to gain access to a kind of Netflix for wrestling, complete with access to the company's extensive video catalogue, original documentaries and other programmes, plus - crucially - live streaming of every pay-per-view. From a viewer's perspective this sounded great: having previously had to pay up to $60 for each month's big show, they were now being told they would get it for less than $10, with unlimited access to hundreds of hours of other content thrown in for free. From

WWE's perspective it made sense too: rather than trying to persuade viewers every month to make a more expensive one-off transaction, why not sign them up to a cheaper subscription whereby most would reliably pay you $120 over the course of a year? Inevitably pay-per-view buys collapsed overnight as fans chose the cheaper option.

At this lower price point WWE hoped that a significantly higher percentage of TV viewers would pay for the Network each month than had previously paid for pay-per-views; in fact the company publicly set a goal of achieving 3 million subscribers worldwide. It never got there: at its peak in 2019 there were around 1.6 million people signed up, far below what they had hoped to achieve. Worse still, the Network had a negative impact on other areas of the business: for example, fewer people were buying DVD releases because they could watch so much content on the Network. The company also sank around $65 million in setup costs for the Network, and its launch affected how much the USA Network offered in 2014 when renewing its TV rights deal - Vince McMahon had said a few months earlier that he was so confident of getting at least double the $77 million per year they were receiving from the previous agreement that he would let a stock analyst put him in a hammerlock if he wasn't proven right. In the event, USA's parent company NBCUniversal was spooked by what the new WWE Network might mean for the future of Raw and Smackdown on regular television, and only agreed to pay around $131 million per year - at least $20 million less than Vince had anticipated. It's not clear whether he was ever put in the hammerlock.

Of course it's impossible to know whether WWE would have made more money in the years after 2014 if it had stuck with traditional pay-per-view instead of launching its own Network, but we do know that pay-per-view did not die in the way that some so-called experts had predicted at the time - on the contrary, events like boxing and UFC have continued to do big numbers. It therefore seems fair to assume that, at the very least, the WWE Network did not bring the kind of transformative change that the company had hoped to achieve when they launched it. Part of the problem there might be to do with the price - some media industry experts have pointed out that charging $9.99 per month was probably too cheap. On-demand services for the most popular US sports were attracting plenty of subscribers at much higher prices, with the NBA charging $36 per month at the time and the NFL going as high as $60 per month. Admittedly WWE didn't have the same level of popularity as those two sports, but there is plenty of reason to believe that they could have raised their price significantly higher - perhaps to the $20 range - without losing too many subscribers. By 2021 the company had apparently concluded that the Network wasn't providing the kind of return on investment that it needed to justify continuing with the experiment, so cashed in by licensing the US rights to NBC streaming service Peacock in a five-year deal worth about $1 billion in total.

RULE OF ENGAGEMENT #16: KNOW THAT A SINGLE MOMENT CAN CHANGE THE ENTIRE WAR

As the wrestling world geared up for WrestleMania 39 in Los Angeles, the wrestling community was rife with speculation regarding the future of WWE, especially in light of Vince McMahon's return to power at the start of the year to explore "strategic alternatives" for the company. The possibility of a sale raised numerous questions about WWE's direction, potential buyers, and the implications for the wrestling industry. The involvement of investment banks and media conglomerates in these discussions hinted at the significant commercial value and global appeal of WWE, making the potential sale a topic of high stakes and widespread interest. If such a story were to break, it would be among the biggest moments in the history of the industry.

The stakes were high creatively for the company too. Roman Reigns' time as WWE's top champion was approaching 1000 days by the time WrestleMania rolled into the City of Angels - a timespan that was almost unfathomable in the fast-moving world of the modern wrestling business. But now, after months of a storyline that was widely regarded as being among the greatest that the promotion had ever produced, it looked as though the final chapter of that story was about to be written: Cody Rhodes was bearing down on Reigns, apparently destined to "finish the story" by winning the most prominent title that his late father never had.

Simultaneously, another big moment was brewing for Cody's former employer. Since its inception, AEW had focused primarily on consolidating its presence in North America. However, as the company grew, so did expectations for its international expansion. Speculation had been mounting about AEW holding its first major show outside of North America, with many eyes set on the United Kingdom, a market with a rich wrestling history and a fervent fan base. Prior to April 2023, there was widespread speculation that AEW would choose Fulham FC's Craven Cottage Stadium for its UK debut, since the Khan family owned the club and its stadium. By the end of WrestleMania week, that assumption had been turned on its head - and so had just about everything else we thought we knew.

CHAPTER 6
THE WEEK THAT SHOOK THE WORLD
ISSUE 49, JUNE 2023
DAVE BRADSHAW

PEOPLE WILL BE TALKING *about the industry-changing events around WrestleMania 39 in Los Angeles for decades to come. Dave Bradshaw has written a first draft of the history of those remarkable few days…*

"This is Hollywood, baby!" exclaimed Carmella as she stood alongside Corey Graves in an empty SoFi Stadium on Friday evening, addressing WWE's YouTube audience. "The stars are gonna be out, there's bound to be a few surprises. It's gonna be bigger than ever!" Moments later, we got the first glimpse of what she meant: the set for WrestleMania 39 was revealed in an explosion of lights and pyrotechnics - and it was immediately apparent that no expense had been spared for this year's Showcase of the Immortals. Inspired by the exterior of an old-school movie theatre, the stage was glistening in gold and placed at the top of a seemingly endless staircase that looked like it was covered in red carpet. To the sides, huge posters inspired by popular blockbusters depicted various WWE talents as major movie stars, and from the centre a long ramp provided the walkway down which wrestlers would make their way to the ring. After a few recent occasions where the WrestleMania stage had felt a little uninspired, this one was instantly among the best in the event's history. The tone had been set: at the most expensive stadium ever built, in the entertainment capital of the world, WWE was about to spend the weekend as the biggest show in town - and it was determined to make the most of the occasion.

This made sense - after all, it was an undeniable fact that this WrestleMania would have more eyes on it than any other in history. As only the second time that the show had been held in front of a full stadium across two nights, the anticipated total of 160,000 attendees was almost certain to be a higher combined number than that managed by any of the event's 38 previous editions. It was also likely to be watched at home by more people than ever, thanks to the fact that NBC's streaming service Peacock, where all WWE Network content is now streamed in the US, had approximately doubled its subscriber numbers over the previous year, with around 20 million customers in the US now having access to the show via their subscriptions. For those reasons alone it made sense for the company to go the extra mile in terms of production and spectacle - but some pundits wondered if there was even more to it than that. As had been well documented, the company was actively seeking "strategic alternatives" - in other words, it was looking for someone to buy it - and this was the weekend above all others when the product could really be shown at its best to potential suitors. Given the Los Angeles location, it was the perfect time to invite bigwigs from major media companies to experience the grandeur of WrestleMania in person and present WWE as an entertainment juggernaut worthy of an enormous asking price.

In the days leading up to WrestleMania there had been increased speculation on that front, driven in part by the news that broke earlier in WrestleMania week about the employment status of Vince McMahon. Three months after he forced his way back onto the company's board of directors, paperwork filed with the US government showed that the company's longtime chairman had now signed a two-year employment contract that would automatically roll on into future years, providing him with a $1.2 million base salary and generous bonuses, as well as a severance package that could be well into seven figures if the company decided to terminate his contract without at least 180 days' notice. This certainly seemed like a sign that McMahon was making it harder to remove himself from the empire he had built, but did it suggest that more substantial news about WWE's future was also imminent? A few financial journalists had started to speculate that such an announcement might not be far away, which made sense given that the review of those "strategic alternatives" had been estimated in January by CEO Nick Khan to last about three months, and to be resolved before the company entered into negotiations about its next TV rights deals later in the spring. Was it possible that there was news being held back until the biggest show of the year was in the rear-view mirror?

Regardless of what was going to happen with WWE, WrestleMania Week had long since become a magnet drawing many of the world's other top wrestling companies to the host city - and this year was no exception. For some of the scene's best wrestlers it can be among the busiest and most physically demanding periods in the calendar: for example, this year Canada's 'Speedball' Mike Bailey had singles matches against Japanese superstars Shigehiro Irie, Kota Ibushi and Hiroshi Tanahashi on three different shows within a six-hour period on Thursday afternoon and evening. The last of those matches took place at a special joint show hosted by Impact Wrestling and New Japan, while other promotions in town included Ring of Honor - nowadays a sister promotion of WWE's main rival All Elite

Wrestling. The week wasn't just about in-ring action either: fan conventions and autograph signings have become a huge element of Mania Week nowadays too. One of the biggest is WrestleCon, which found itself at the centre of an unpleasant controversy on Friday: Impact's Gisele Shaw, who came out as a transgender woman in 2022, reported via her Instagram that evening that she had been subjected to a volley of verbal transphobic abuse at the event from veteran wrestler Rick Steiner. In response to the allegations WrestleCon put out a statement apologising to Shaw, and Steiner was reportedly barred from the remainder of the convention. The wrestling community mostly rallied around Shaw, but it was still an ugly episode in a week that was meant to be a celebration of everything great about professional wrestling.

Luckily there was plenty worth celebrating, not least at WWE's annual Hall of Fame ceremony on Friday night, held at the Crypto.com Arena (formerly the Staples Center) immediately after the go-home episode of SmackDown. This year's class included posthumous inductions for comedian Andy Kaufman and referee Tim White, while Attitude Era star Stacy Keibler and recently-retired Japanese legend The Great Muta were able to collect their honours in person. The headliner of the Class of 2023 was Rey Mysterio, whose entrance was brilliantly worked to play into the build to his match with son Dominik the following night: as the older Mysterio made his way to the ring, Dominik and his pals from Judgment Day stood up and walked out of the arena in a delicious gesture of disrespect. That infusion of a storyline on a night where wrestlers are mostly 'out of character' was a reminder of how, at its best, our artform can blur the line between fact and fiction better than any other. The ceremony was also newsworthy for another reason: it provided the first photographic evidence of Vince McMahon's rumoured moustache, revealing that the industry's most powerful figure had now opted for a look akin to the kind of vaudeville villain who might have just tied a damsel to the railroad tracks. Bizarre.

By the time the sun rose on the City of Angels for WrestleMania Saturday, fans everywhere were amped up for a card that most agreed had the potential to be one of the best that the company had ever put together. Regardless of the recent boardroom turmoil, WWE's on-screen product had been much improved in recent months: in particular, the months-long storyline pitting top heel group The Bloodline against Sami Zayn, Kevin Owens and Cody Rhodes was considered to be some of the best creative work the company had ever produced. Cody's chance at ending the record-breaking world title run of Bloodline leader Roman Reigns would wait until Sunday; Saturday was all about KO and Sami challenging the Usos in an effort to overthrow the longest-reigning tag team champions in the promotion's history. But would this be the main event of night one, or would that honour go to Charlotte Flair and Rhea Ripley's battle for the SmackDown Women's Championship? It was apparent during the week that no final decision had been made in that regard, and both sides made their case as the big night approached: when Zayn was asked about it by ESPN he said that the tag title storyline "has spoken for itself at this point", while Flair suggested on journalist Ryan Satin's podcast that the winner of the men's Royal Rumble gets to main event WrestleMania 99.9% of the time, and questioned why the same is not true of the women's Royal Rumble now that WrestleMania is over two nights and can have two main events. While it isn't true overall that the men's Rumble winners have anything close to a 100% record of main eventing WrestleMania, Cody's match against Reigns would be the fourth year in a row that the men's winner had closed one of Mania's two nights, while only two of the five women's winners had headlined since the women's rumble started in 2018.

While the main event of night one might have been shrouded in mystery, there were no such doubts around which match would be opening the show: WWE had already announced that Austin Theory was set to raise the curtain with his US title defence against 16-time world champion John Cena, who would be participating in his first regular in-ring Mania match for five years. Before that, NXT held their show case Stand and Deliver event over at the Crypto.com Arena in the afternoon, headlined by Carmelo Hayes taking the NXT Championship from Bron Breakker - who, as Rick Steiner's son, had presumably been through an interesting 24 hours. After that show, fans began making their way into SoFi Stadium which somehow looked even more breathtaking in the daylight - this was the fourth time that WrestleMania had taken place in LA (or the sixth if you count Anaheim as being part of the Los Angeles area), but the first to be held in a stadium - and it was certainly a setting that was fit for the occasion. Somehow this felt grander than other recent WrestleManias - and by the end of the weekend it would come to feel like, for better or worse, it was an era-defining moment.

A FLAWLESS FIRST NIGHT

The main show began with the obligatory rendition of America The Beautiful, this time from recording artist Becky G, before Hollywood star Kevin Hart narrated a hype video, and a brief in-ring welcome from The Miz and Snoop Dogg, who must hold some kind of record by now for the most celebrity appearances at WrestleMania. Cena, whose 600 visits with Make-A-Wish kids is certainly a record, had some of them join him on stage for his entrance in a genuinely moving moment to start the show. "You'd better win!" shouted one of the kids at Cena as he started his charge down the ramp to the ring, and 80,000 fans inside the stadium gave the company's biggest star of the 21st Century a welcome that was warmer than most he had received during his tenure as a full-time talent. The crowd were probably not the only ones who were appreciated Cena that day - for Austin Theory this was undoubtedly the biggest match of his career so far, and there had been no guarantee in the months before WrestleMania that he would be the one granted the opportunity, with Logan Paul and Cody Rhodes also reportedly touted within the company as potential opponents. Theory had absorbed some devastating put-downs in a Raw promo by Cena leading up to the show, but there was never much doubt what the purpose of this match was: in a basic but fun match lasting just over 10 minutes, Cena ended up looking at the lights to give Theory the 'rub' that might help boost him towards the top of the card.

A raucous four-way tag team match won by the Street Profits provided a wildly entertaining second match on the show, before Logan Paul and Seth Rollins arrived for a match that many expected could steal the show. Both men had plenty of motivation: for all of his critics, Paul's four previous outings had already secured his place as the best in-ring performer of all the celebrities who have ever made the crossover into the squared circle, but he was undoubtedly eager to cement that position against an opponent whom many expected would get the best out of him. Rollins himself seemed determined to make a point, having recently told ESPN that he was unhappy about the idea of Cody Rhodes getting to main event WrestleMania instead of him. "I feel, based on my body of work and what I've contributed to this company over the course of this last decade, I should be in that position," he had said. "I put my head down, I work hard, I vouch for this company. I feel like, what he [Cody] is getting..I'm just not entirely comfortable with it."

Whatever was driving both men, it led to something pretty special in SoFi Stadium. Paul's elaborate entrance included him flying above the crowd in a harness before walking down the ramp accompanied by a mascot dressed as a bottle of his Prime sports drink. Rollins' entrance involved the crowd being led in singing his theme by an actual conductor, as the pageantry of WrestleMania started to kick into high gear. Inevitably as the match unfolded the Prime mascot became involved, and we found out that the man inside the bottle was Paul's business partner and fellow influencer KSI, who shortly afterwards ended up being put through a table courtesy of a Logan Paul frog splash that had been intended for Rollins. A few moments and a curb stomp later, Rollins claimed victory in a match that somehow managed to exceed the high expectations many had held for it. WrestleMania 39 was off to a flyer.

The six-woman tag match that followed was a solid bout that served its purpose, and it was great to see Trish Stratus and Lita back in a WrestleMania ring as they teamed with Becky Lynch to defeat Damage CTRL. After that came the father-versus-son clash between Rey and Dominik Mysterio, which created an unlikely controversy of its own. Dominik's entrance was for the most part a work of comic genius, as he was shown being released from a prison cell, handcuffed and transported in a van to the stadium, where he was escorted to the ring by correctional officers. Unfortunately, though, the video contained some stock footage of the outside of a prison that turned out to have been taken at the Auschwitz concentration camp. The historic site's Twitter account commented on the incident in the days after the show, expressing scepticism that the inclusion of the footage had been a simple editing mistake and adding: "Exploiting the site that became a symbol of enormous human tragedy is shameless and insults the memory of all victims of Auschwitz." WWE apologised and told the Washington Post: "We had no knowledge of what was depicted. As soon as we learned, it was removed immediately."

Rey's entrance was far less contentious, as he paid tribute to the late Eddie Guerrero by arriving in a low-rider that was driven by Snoop Dogg because of course it was. 15 minutes later, after a fun brawl between Dominik and Rey, the older Mysterio got the win when his son's efforts to use a steel chain were thwarted by music megastar Bad Bunny, who had joined the Spanish announce team on commentary for the match. The finish was clearly designed to set up a match at Backlash in early May, where Bad Bunny would be the event host in his native Puerto Rico, but that didn't matter - this match was another great addition to what was quickly becoming a near-flawless first night. Little did we know that things were about to get even better.

The question of which match would main event was answered by the fact that Flair and Ripley were next to the ring. Perhaps, like Rollins, these two wanted to make a statement after being overlooked for the closing spot on the show - and they certainly achieved that goal. An utterly compelling back-and-forth that lasted close to 25 minutes, this was arguably a top-ten match in WrestleMania history. By the time Ripley won with a Riptide from the turnbuckle, having escaped Charlotte's figure-eight leglock, there wasn't a person in the building who could doubt the main event credentials of either woman. Very few matches could have followed it, but fan interest in the story between Owens, Zayn and the Bloodline was at such a fever pitch that it still somehow felt right that they should have the chance to present a first-ever tag title main event at WrestleMania. Michael Cole, who was setting a record over the weekend by commentating his 22nd WrestleMania, had given the storyline high praise in a podcast interview earlier in the week. "It's incredible," he said. "This story is the best story that I've been involved in for 26 years. Bar none, by far, for so many different reasons... This story deserves an Emmy, or at least a nomination."

After a brief filler segment where Snoop Dogg (who else?) convinced Miz to wrestle an impromptu match against Pat McAfee, the main event took to the ring and told a story that was made for the occasion, with the Usos dominating for long periods before Owens and Zayn came back to claim the win. Sami's pinfall over Jey Uso to win it was followed by a thunderous roar as good as any in WrestleMania history. Some people were in tears from the sheer emotion the match and its build had conjured up. This was close to sports entertainment perfection, and as WrestleMania 39's first night went off air, there was a clear case for declaring it the best night of action in the event's history. If night two could match it then surely most fans would agree that WrestleMania X-Seven had finally been dethroned as the greatest of all time. But before the second half of the show could even get underway, a story developed that ensured this year's WrestleMania would happen at a moment that was every bit as consequential as that landmark event in 2001, which was held less than a week after Vince McMahon purchased WCW.

THE UNPREDICTABLE ENCORE

On the afternoon of Sunday 2nd April, shortly before fans started returning to SoFi Stadium for night two, CNBC broke the story that WWE was "in advanced talks to be sold to Ari Emanuel's Endeavor Group, the parent company of UFC", with a deal due to be announced potentially the following day. In fact the two companies were far beyond "advanced talks", as Emanuel and Vince McMahon had already pre-recorded an interview with CNBC to announce the deal - the details of which we have covered extensively elsewhere in this issue. As you might expect, the notion that Vince McMahon was giving up control of his empire after four decades was momentous in any circumstances, but coming in the middle of one of the biggest events in company history lent that Sunday a surreal edge that had never quite been felt before. At SoFi Stadium there was a palpable sense that the 80,000 who had shown up for night two were convening as a fanbase not just for a night of in-ring action, but to jointly experience one of the most consequential moments in wrestling history.

Against that backdrop it felt oddly difficult to get into the first two matches of the evening: Brock Lesnar's win over Omos was passable and didn't outstay its welcome, while the four-way women's tag match that followed it was also solid without being memorable. People's minds were somehow elsewhere, and it was only when the intercontinental title match got underway that the action drew everyone back in. Gunther, Sheamus and Drew McIntyre beat the ever-living hell out of each other in a war that may be remembered in time as having done a great deal to restore the prestige of the championship - after all, it had been a long time since there had been a genuine classic for that belt on WWE's grandest stage, and the previous year it hadn't even made the card at all. Gunther ultimately won here after powerbombing both his opponents, and remained on track to possibly beat Honky Tonk Man's long-standing record for the longest reign in the title's 44-year history.

Bianca Belair and Asuka put on a very good match for the Raw Women's Championship next, in which Belair retained the title and completed a full year as champion. A particularly poignant story emerged after the show about the champ's entrance: Belair had been accompanied by a local dance troupe called 'The Divas of Compton', and Triple H revealed at the post-show press conference that the little girl from the group who had a starring role in the routine had found out that her mother had died just hours before the performance. It was a jaw-dropping revelation that cast the entrance in a whole new light, and made it a truly special WrestleMania moment. Another memorable moment followed, albeit for entirely different reasons: for the second night in a row the Miz was due to face a mystery opponent and, to everyone's surprise, that opponent was Shane McMahon. But moments into the two men's match, McMahon tore his quad while performing a simple leapfrog, and was unable to continue. Who could possibly step up to save this segment on the fly? Snoop Dogg, that's who! Apparently improvising, Snoop knocked Miz down a couple of times, hit his own version of the People's Elbow, and secured the victory in a match where he wasn't even one of the competitors. Shane's mishap oddly turned the segment into something that many of us will remember for a long time - sometimes the best moments are the ones that aren't manufactured at all.

It speaks a lot to how stacked the WrestleMania card was this year that a Hell In A Cell match - the first on the show in seven years - really wasn't among its most talked-about attractions, but Edge and Finn Balor put on an excellent hardcore battle within the confines of the huge structure, which thankfully had been returned to its original metallic colour after several years of being painted blood-red. Speaking of blood, Balor suffered a head wound mid-match that briefly stopped the action and looked particularly gruesome, but was able to continue and get his storyline comeuppance by suffering the same fate as that to which he had subjected Edge's wife Beth Phoenix: a Conchairto to the skull. The only downside to this match was that it involved lengthy gaps in action before and afterwards while the cell was moved and the ring cleared. But no matter, because the WWE Universe was gearing up for the climax of a story that had been running for close to three years: after 945 days, a length of time almost unfathomable in the modern wrestling industry with its weekly TV shows and monthly premium events, was Roman Reigns about to lose his world titles? Was Cody Rhodes about to do what his father had never been able to do in WWE, and win the big one? Would the American Nightmare finish the story? Surely he would... right?

Most readers will know what happened next: despite an all-time classic WrestleMania main event, Reigns unexpectedly pinned Rhodes after interference from Solo Sikoa. The reaction inside the stadium was one of legitimate shock, perhaps more so than any outcome since Brock Lesnar ended the Undertaker's streak nine years earlier. If now was not the time and place to pull the trigger on a title change, when on Earth was? Had this been a stroke of booking genius, or had WWE just fumbled a moment that could have been one of the most feelgood it had ever produced? Was this a sign that Vince McMahon had his claws firmly back into the creative process and had swiftly destroyed all the good will that Triple H had spent the last several months building?

THE NEVERENDING STORY

As it turned out, the answer to that last question was apparently no. Reports quickly emerged that plans for Reigns to win the match had quietly been in place for several weeks and that McMahon had not been the one to make the decision. At the post-show press conference Triple H said of the decision: "If I didn't feel like we had a compelling story on the other side, it wouldn't be the decision." His choice was later backed up by Paul Heyman, who had been one of the key characters in the story arc and is considered by many in the industry to be a master booker. Heyman described the match and its outcome as "storytelling at its very best" and argued that the result only wants fans even more desperate to see Cody dethrone his rival. "You go for the biggest box office," he told BT Sport's Ariel Helwani. "It's a business. When will people be at their peak of the desire to see Cody challenge again for the championship to such a degree that they're willing to pay the most money to see it happen?" Plenty of others disagreed: among them was Kurt Angle, who said he felt ratings would go down as a result of the finish because the title had now been kept on Reigns for a length of time that was not palatable to a modern audience.

The anger among some fans at the finish would only get worse 24 hours later. As expected, the news was confirmed on Monday that WWE was indeed merging with Endeavor, and in the CNBC interview Vince McMahon claimed he would no longer be getting "in the weeds" of the day-to-day creative process. That claim was called into question just hours later, however, when the episode of Monday Night Raw after WrestleMania - considered one of the most important shows of the year - had Vince's fingerprints all over it. There were reports of the production team being handed multiple last-minute changes to the format for the show, including matches being changed or replaced entirely, and McMahon apparently spent the night at the 'gorilla position' by the stage, increasingly taking charge of the show as it proceeded. For many fans and apparently at least some members of the roster, this development was deeply concerning, and some wrestlers told journalists anonymously that they would be considering whether to ask for their releases if he continued to be involved on that level.

With discontent apparently rising, WWE's main rival could not have timed their own big announcement any better. On Wednesday's edition of Dynamite, just three days after WrestleMania and two days after that badly received episode of Raw, Tony Khan revealed that his company would be making its UK debut in August, and had booked the iconic Wembley Stadium for the occasion. Given the building's

90,000 capacity this was among the most audacious moves that Khan could have made, and speculation immediately turned to how many tickets they might be able to sell. On the same episode of Dynamite, former New Japan star Jay White was revealed as the latest member of the AEW roster, after WWE's efforts to sign him had stalled. Many saw this as a sign that things might not be boding well for WWE: after several months of critical acclaim and rising ratings, was it again becoming the case that major stars were thinking twice about entering the McMahon orbit, especially when there was such a well-funded and ambitious alternative? Had WWE once again ceded the initiative in its ongoing war with AEW?

At the time of writing we still don't know the answers to any of those questions. However, what we certainly know is that by the morning of Thursday 6th April, as the news of AEW's Wembley announcement was making the rounds, the entire wrestling world felt like it was in a completely different place to where it had been just seven days earlier. Think about it: on the Thursday before WrestleMania, ownership of WWE was still firmly in Vince McMahon's hands, he was not believed to be heavily involved in creative, and many fans were confident that they were about to witness the end of Roman Reigns' time as champion. Jay White was widely expected to sign with the company and maybe even show up at WrestleMania, while AEW had largely been pushed into the background as the biggest weekend of the year approached. Shane McMahon still had a fully functioning quadricep, and Snoop Dogg did not have any WrestleMania victories to his name. None of that was true just one week later, and instead we found ourselves entering a strange new world after a breathless few days that will be talked about for decades to come. Everything was different now, and goodness only knew what was coming next. Perhaps Triple H summed up the reality of the wrestling industry in 2023 at that post-show press conference, where his words about the

Cody-Roman match could equally be applied to the twists and turns that continue to take palace off-camera: "The story never finishes… we just got to the end of the chapter. The story continues and that's where this gets interesting to me. That is what is the most amazing thing about our business, the story never ends."

RULE OF ENGAGEMENT #17: BE PREPARED TO MOUNT A BLOODLESS COUP IF NECESSARY

The merger between WWE and Endeavor didn't emerge from a vacuum. It was the climax of a long-standing and complex relationship between two of the entertainment industry's most influential brands. The ties between the two dated back to various key interactions and mutual business interests through the years, including their cooperation with regard to talent such as Brock Lesnar and Ronda Rousey, as both switched between the two companies. Moreover, Vince McMahon and Ari Emanuel shared a common vision in terms of content distribution and media rights strategies. Both WWE and UFC had successfully transitioned into the digital space with their respective streaming services, WWE Network and UFC Fight Pass, at around the same time in early 2014 and late 2013 respectively.

The merger, therefore, seemed like a natural progression of the relationship between two men who had great respect for each other. It was built on a foundation of prior collaborations, mutual business interests, and a shared vision for the future of sports entertainment and media. That was one way to look at it - and undoubtedly the way that both men would have liked the story to be told.

But was that the full story? Were both men being completely candid in their joint TV interview after announcing the merger - or was one man playing checkers while the other was playing chess? These were some of the questions being asked in the aftermath of April's bombshell announcement, and events since then have only made those questions seem more relevant. The early analysis of the deal took place while pundits didn't necessarily have all of the facts at their disposal, but that doesn't necessarily mean that their hunches were wrong...

CHAPTER 7
THE FINAL DAYS OF VINCE MCMAHON
ISSUE 49, JUNE 2023
DAVE BRADSHAW

HAS WWE's kingpin just made the ultimate power play, or has he been duped into handing over the keys to his empire? Dave Bradshaw looks at how the merger with Endeavor will define the legacy of professional wrestling's most influential figure…

It was quite a morning. Just hours after the curtain fell on the biggest and most controversial WrestleMania of all time, WWE chairman Vince McMahon was on television with Ari Emanuel, the CEO of UFC's parent company Endeavor, announcing that the two companies were merging. Sat next to each other on CNBC, they were being quizzed on various elements of the deal including what would happen if the two men disagreed on any major decisions. Emanuel responded to the question by describing the deal as a partnership in which the two men would work together through any difficulties. McMahon reacted to this jokily: "Let me make it clear… I thought you worked for me?"

The awkward laughter that immediately ensued was perhaps the most interesting moment of the entire 16-minute interview. It seemed to betray a sense that, actually, it wasn't entirely clear what would happen if the two men disagreed. Under the terms of the deal, UFC and WWE would break off from Endeavor and form a new entity. 51% of this new business would be owned by existing Endeavor shareholders and 49% by WWE shareholders, while the board of directors would consist of six executives from Endeavor and five from WWE. Emanuel would be the CEO of the new company and McMahon would be executive chairman of the board... so which one of them was actually in charge?

In many corporate structures the executive chairman is generally deemed the top dog rather than the CEO, but that couldn't be right in this case: after all Endeavor were the senior partners percentage-wise, and the deal valued UFC at over $12 billion while WWE was a little over $9 billion. Moreover, when the merger is completed (probably in late 2023), McMahon will find for the first time in over 40 years that he does not have majority voting rights in his company: his WWE shares will only convert into about 18% ownership of the new venture and - unlike his current arrangement - his shares won't give him any greater voting power than any other shareholder. McMahon will be a minority shareholder, and his people will be in a minority on the board of directors.

So, does that mean Emanuel will effectively outrank McMahon? Not according to the man himself: in the CNBC interview Emanuel said he would leave the day-to-day running of WWE from a creative standpoint to McMahon, just as he leaves the running of UFC to its president Dana White. However, what wasn't quite so clear from his answer was whether the same hands-off approach would apply when it came to bigger decisions that might affect the company as a whole rather than just the WWE brand. "If we disagree on something we want to do, guess what, we're not doing it," Emanuel said. "But if there's a disagreement, that's called a relationship. We will work it out." This was the moment at which McMahon made his joke about Emanuel working for him. You could be forgiven for thinking that he was being a little bit more serious than either man would have cared to admit.

Certainly, one of those who felt as though things were not entirely as they seemed in the interview was reporter Alex Sherman, who had broken the news of the merger during WrestleMania weekend. "It's all a show," he said of the interview when speaking to Wrestlenomics the following day. "The whole thing has been a work, just like WWE is. Do I believe that Ari Emanuel and Vince McMahon are just not going to do anything if they disagree? Of course I don't. There's going to have to be some kind of pecking order there, and I think that's a really valid potential thorny thing."

That part of the interview wasn't the only section that Sherman and others found to be somewhat implausible. From the moment the cameras started rolling, it was clear that one of the main messages Emanuel wanted to convey was his admiration for Vince McMahon, describing him as a visionary who had been ahead of the curve in his industry for decades. When asked directly if he wanted Vince to stay active in the company as part of the deal, Emanuel was emphatic: "Oh my God yes… I would have body-slammed him if he thought he was going to leave!"

While there is arguably nothing odd about praising the bold decisions that McMahon had made in building his company over the years, Emanuel's enthusiasm for him staying on after the merger is reportedly in stark contrast to how almost every other possible buyer viewed the situation. Sean Ross Sapp of Fightful had spoken with executives at most of the potential suitors during the past few months and reported that they had almost all told him that McMahon's continued involvement in the company was deemed a liability rather than an asset, and made them less likely to bid for the company.

The reasons are not rocket science: most importantly, since last summer McMahon has been embroiled in a scandal surrounding alleged sexual misconduct and hush money payments. The allegations led him to "retire", only to reinstall himself as chairman of the board in January. Quite aside from the sordid nature of the claims and the reputational impact that this might have on any company with which McMahon is associated, there is another reason that this episode might put off potential bidders: the company did not stumble without him in charge. On the contrary, during his half-year absence live event attendance and TV ratings improved, as did the critical reception to the company's TV product. The common wisdom had always been that Vince McMahon was the beating heart of WWE and that it could not survive without him - but those months without him at the wheel had demonstrated that this was simply no longer true.

FUTURE ENDEAVORS

With the benefit of hindsight, perhaps Endeavor were always therefore among the frontrunners to acquire WWE since they were one of the only contenders who were willing to countenance McMahon's continued involvement. The agreement they struck was a stock deal rather than a cash deal - in other words, Endeavor did not pay a single dollar to Vince McMahon or any other WWE shareholder to acquire the company. Instead they "paid" the shareholders by converting their WWE shares into shares in the new entity that is being formed. There is thus no guarantee that WWE shareholders make any significant profit from the deal - the hope is that the new company is more profitable than WWE would have been if it had continued to go it alone, so the value of the shares will rise. However, in terms of providing immediate "value", a cash deal would have been more profitable in the short term since shareholders would have had their shares bought from them and received a cash payout.

Of course, a cash deal would have meant that Vince McMahon was simply bought out of his own company, and the new owners would have been under no obligation to keep him on as executive chairman or any other role. Instead, by striking a stock deal, McMahon was able to negotiate a major role for himself within the new entity: he will still own nearly a fifth of the company, and he will still be chairman of the board. It seems likely that maintaining this power was more attractive to him than getting a multi-billion dollar payout and spending the rest of his life on a beach enjoying his retirement.

If this is true then the only bidders who could ever have been considered were those willing to offer a stock deal. Among those who it probably eliminated were Comcast, the owners of NBCUniversal. They were seen as possible suitors since their USA Network is the home channel for Monday Night Raw in the US, and their Peacock streaming service already hosts the WWE Network in the country too. Some people speculated that rather than paying hundreds of millions of dollars in a new TV rights deal to be negotiated later this year, they might prefer to simply buy the company outright. However, it seems unlikely that a bombastic personality like McMahon would ever have been a good fit for a large corporate structure like Comcast's, so they were always unlikely to do a deal that kept McMahon involved.

In fact, even if a cash deal had been an option there is some doubt that they would have been interested: the value of big media companies has decreased in the past year, meaning that there is less money flying around for acquisitions - and in any case, Comcast reportedly has its eyes on buying streaming service Hulu or possibly even on a merger between NBC Universal and Warner Bros Discovery. A purchase of WWE, which might have cost $9 billion, was probably always a low priority compared to those possible deals. The same may have been true of other big corporations who might have been interested: the likes of Disney and Apple may have similarly found a stock deal unappealing and a cash deal unaffordable. Another potential buyer was the Saudi Arabian government (indeed they were falsely rumoured to be on the brink of completing a deal in January), but in their case only a cash deal seems likely, and then McMahon would not have retained any control.

So why was Ari Emanuel prepared to keep McMahon in the fold when most other potential buyers were not? One reason might be that he genuinely believes what he said in the CNBC interview - that McMahon is a visionary and the company will be better off with him involved. Another factor might be that he doesn't see the scandal surrounding McMahon as being a critical problem. Earlier this year UFC president Dana White escaped punishment from higher-ups at Endeavor when footage emerged of him slapping his wife during an argument at a new year's party. While that is obviously an entirely different situation to the allegations surrounding McMahon, it does suggest at the very least that Emanuel is not one to offload key members of his team in the face of bad publicity. Instead, McMahon was permitted to brush aside the allegations surrounding him with a quick answer during the CNBC interview: "I've made mistakes obviously, both personally and professionally, during my 50-year career. I've owned up to every single one of them, and then moved on." Whether that is the final word on the matter remains to be seen.

Another theory, proposed by Fightful founder Jimmy Van among others during analysis in the days following the deal's announcement, is that Emanuel is fully aware of the problems involved in keeping McMahon active in the new company but expects that he will soon be gone. Under this theory, the constant stroking of McMahon's ego in the CNBC interview might have been part of a deliberate ploy by Emanuel to ensure that Endeavor won the battle to acquire WWE. Then, although McMahon would temporarily be chairman of the board, he could be ousted early in the life of the new company. The typical pattern for most corporations is to elect people to positions on the board annually, and of course Endeavor will have more of its people on the new board than WWE will so they could easily vote McMahon out of his position within a year or two. In fact, it's not even clear that the five board members from the WWE side would unanimously support McMahon continuing as executive chairman. Perhaps then, Emanuel and the other key players in the deal believe that they will be able to oust McMahon soon after the deal is concluded.

But hold on a second. If wrestling journalists have been able to identify this as a possibility then it seems unlikely that the same thought wouldn't have crossed Vince's own mind before he agreed to the deal. At the time of writing we are yet to see what provisions (if any) are included that might reassure McMahon that he won't be ousted from the board at the first opportunity. What we do know, however, is that in the week before the deal was announced WWE filed paperwork showing that McMahon had agreed to a new two-year employment contract for his role as executive chairman. Again, we don't know the full terms of that contract, but might it include provisions that would make it almost impossible to get rid of him? For example, there has been some speculation that the contract might include a severance package that would make it prohibitively expensive for the company to relieve Vince of his duties during the next two years.

AN ENDING STILL UNWRITTEN

Perhaps, then, it is not so likely after all that there are plans afoot to oust Vince from the new company shortly after the merger is completed. This might come as something of a disappointment to the legions of WWE fans who have been upset to see McMahon return to the company this year, and were particularly annoyed to see his fingerprints all over the episode of Monday Night Raw that aired on the same day that the deal was announced. Many had very much preferred the company's on-screen product during the months that Triple H had been in charge, and fear a return to the 'bad old days' of McMahon's often frustrating style of storytelling if he is making a permanent return to the company's creative team. However, there are at least three other scenarios that might result in McMahon leaving the stage sooner than expected.

The first relates to the fact that Vince is not a young man. While he currently seems to be in excellent health for a man of his 77 years, there comes a time when everyone is forced to slow down a bit - even those most wedded to their work. It might well be that as McMahon reaches the end of his eighth decade he really will avoid getting "in the weeds" of everyday operations at WWE, as he suggested would be the case in the CNBC interview. Admittedly the early signs were not encouraging in that regard, given that Vince was heavily involved in Monday Night Raw within literally hours of the interview airing - but he mostly kept away from that Friday's Smackdown and the following week's Raw in Seattle, so his level of involvement remains an open question.

The second scenario that might see McMahon take a backseat is that we still have no idea how he will cope with being part of a corporate structure where he is not the lord and master of all he surveys. Let's assume for a moment that there is no grand conspiracy whereby the rest of the board plan to oust Vince at the first possible opportunity. Even if that is the case, and Emanuel really does want to form a long-term working partnership with him, there's no way of knowing how Vince will interact in an environment among other alpha males where he has equal or less power than others in the room. Is this a tinderbox waiting to explode? And if it did emerge that the new company wasn't big enough for the larger-than-life personalities of Emanuel, White, McMahon and others, who would win that boardroom battle? It is far from certain that it would be Vince who survived.

Thirdly, and perhaps most worryingly from McMahon's perspective, we still do not know if last year's scandal is fully resolved. After the conclusion of an internal investigation into the alleged hush money payments, in March Vince paid the company $17.4 million to cover any costs the company had incurred. He will be hoping that this is the end of the matter, but we don't know if federal prosecutors are still looking into it (they apparently were as recently as December), or whether any charges will be brought. We also don't know if any other accusations will come to light, although a letter from the other board members to Vince on 27th December last year may provide some interesting insight. In recommending that he stay away from involvement in the company, they wrote that his return "would not be prudent from a shareholder value perspective. This determination is based on a variety of factors, including non-public information the Board has become aware of and the risks to the Company and its shareholders of placing a greater spotlight on these issues." We still don't know what this 'non-public information' might be and whether it bears any relevance. Of course, in January McMahon was able to ignore the board's advice and force his way back into the fold because ultimately he had the voting power to unilaterally do so - but after the merger is completed that power will be gone, and if the other directors on the new company's board decided his issues were causing too much aggravation then it's not inconceivable that they could move to eject him.

Ultimately though, this is all guesswork. We simply do not know yet how Vince McMahon's story will end - but interestingly, we do know who will get to write that story. The new two-year employment deal that McMahon recently signed with WWE includes a stipulation that he will retain the rights to his own intellectual property, meaning that even if he later leaves the company, he will have sole control over licensing any books, movies or other media that tell his life story. Many former WWE wrestlers might raise an eyebrow at this, given that the rights to tell their stories have routinely been withheld by WWE long after their time in the company is over. Vince will not be bound by any such restrictions, meaning that he will have significant control over how the official version of his legacy is presented.

But what about unofficially? That might well depend on how this all plays out: perhaps Vince McMahon really has played the situation perfectly, navigating his way out of a scandal to become even wealthier than he was before, winning back his job in the process and becoming more powerful than ever in the world of professional sports and entertainment. Alternatively, perhaps his ego has finally got the better of him, allowing him to be sweet-talked into a deal that will rapidly see him booted out of the empire he built. Maybe his health, his fellow board members or a new wave of scandals might finally see him meet his match - or perhaps another option that we simply have not considered. Whatever happens, one big question still needs to be answered: what will all of this mean for WWE, both in these last chapters of the Vince McMahon era and after he finally, once and for all, rides off into the sunset?

THE LOW-DOWN ON ENDEAVOR

Endeavor launched as a Hollywood talent agency in 1995, founded by Ari Emanuel and three business partners with offices in Beverly Hills. The company spent the next several years building a reputation for "quick thinking, ferocity and barely bridled ambition", as described by the New York Times in 2009. During the 2000s it built up a formidable roster of clients including Ben Affleck, Matt Damon, Christian Bale, Hugh Jackman and Adam Sandler - it also became the inspiration for the TV show Entourage, with main character Ari Gold being based on Ari Emanuel.

In 2009 Endeavor merged with another one called the William Morris Agency, a world-famous company that had been around for over a hundred years and represented the likes of Charlie Chaplin, the Beach Boys and the Rolling Stones. The new company, William Morris Endeavor (WME) continued to go from strength to strength and Emanuel was included in Fortune magazine's Businesspeople of the Year list in 2010. The company expanded into social media management, digital advertising and e-commerce, and in 2013 it teamed up with a private equity firm to acquire International Management Group (IMG), a sports events and production company, for a fee of $2.4 billion.

The acquisitions kept coming: rodeo company Professional Bull Riders was added to the fold in 2015, as was the Miss Universe Organisation - which they bought from Donald Trump, who was a former client of theirs. Emanuel's business relationship with Trump is particularly interesting, since Trump was by this point running to be the Republican candidate for president, while Emanuel is the younger brother of prominent Democrat Rahm Emanuel, who was Chief of Staff to President Barack Obama in the White House and then went on to be the mayor of Chicago. Ari himself has held fundraising events for the Democrats and donated to Hillary Clinton's presidential campaign in 2016, but also reportedly offered to assist Trump's campaign in the same election.

In 2016 Endeavor made its biggest acquisition yet, buying the Ultimate Fighting Championship (UFC) for just over $4 billion, which was a record amount in professional sports. A couple of years later Endeavor was in the news again, this time because it was moving to extricate itself from a $400 million investment by the Saudi government in the wake of the state-sponsored murder of journalist Jamal Khassoghi. Given this friction with the Saudi regime, it is not entirely clear whether WWE's deal with the country might become more difficult following the upcoming merger.

In 2019 Endeavor announced its intention to become a publicly traded company, but postponed the plan just one day before they were due to float on the New York Stock Exchange to "evaluate the timing for the proposed offering as market conditions develop". In March 2021 the plan to go public was revived and Elon Musk joined its board of directors, although he resigned in 2022. The company started being publicly traded on 28th April 2021, and by the time of the proposed merger with WWE it was valued at around $12 billion. By the time the merger was announced Endeavor and WWE had already been working together for four years, as Endeavor Streaming had been providing backend services for the WWE Network since 2019.

THE TIMELINE

May 19, 2022 - Stephanie McMahon announces she is taking a leave of absence from WWE.

June 15, 2022 - The Wall Street Journal publishes an article claiming WWE is investigating Vince McMahon for an alleged $3 million hush money settlement allegedly paid to a former employee.

June 17, 2022 - Vince McMahon steps back from leadership roles while investigation is conducted, but remains in charge of creative. Stephanie McMahon returns as interim chairwoman and CEO.

July 8, 2022 - A second Wall Street Journal article is published, alleging Vince McMahon paid $12 million in hush money to four separate women.

July 22, 2022 - Vince McMahon announces he has taken the decision to retire from WWE. Stephanie McMahon is named permanent chairwoman of WWE.

July 25, 2022 - Triple H is named head of WWE's creative team.

August 8, 2023 - John Laurinaitis is sacked by WWE.

August 9, 2023 - WWE reveals Vince McMahon made undisclosed payments totalling $19.6 million to settle sexual misconduct claims made between 2006 and 2022.

December 20, 2022 - Vince McMahon writes a letter to the board of WWE, indicating he is looking to return to the company.

December 27, 2023 - The WWE board responds to Vince McMahon's letter, stating the belief is that his return to the company at that time would not be prudent.

January 6, 2023 - Vince McMahon ignores the board and returns to WWE anyway, allegedly to oversee a potential sale of the company. Claims he will not have an impact on creative.

January 10, 2023 - Stephanie McMahon resigns as WWE Chairman, and Vince McMahon is elected executive chairman of WWE soon after.

January 19, 2023 - Vince McMahon settles out of court with former WWE referee who alleged sexual misconduct against him.

February 28, 2023 - Brock Lesnar vs. Omos announced for

WrestleMania 39, escalating rumours Vince McMahon is back in creative.

March 6, 2023 - Vince McMahon spotted backstage, talent reveal he's grown a "creepy little moustache".

March 31, 2023 - Vince McMahon reportedly signs new 2-year deal with WWE.

Vince helping creative

April 3, 2023 - WWE reaches an agreement to be sold to UFC parent company Endeavour.

April 4, 2023 - New report claims Vince McMahon is "firmly back in charge" of WWE creative, despite his initial promises that he wouldn't do exactly that. Numerous reports claiming Vince is making several changes to every single week of WWE TV.

RULE OF ENGAGEMENT #18: OPEN A NEW FRONT IN THE WAR IF CIRCUMSTANCES WARRANT IT

If your TV show ain't big enough for the both of them, get another TV show! That might be a slightly flippant way to look at Tony Khan's solution to his CM Punk problem in the summer of 2023, but the deal to bring AEW Collision to TNT from June certainly had the added benefit of providing a way to keep Punk away from The Elite while having him return from his suspension. When Khan announced that the inaugural episode of Collision would be at Chicago's United Center and that Punk would be a part of it, the logic of the decision wasn't difficult to decipher.

Indeed, Punk was to be the centrepiece of the new show, working mostly alongside talent with whom he was on good terms, and thereby creating a sort of quasi-brand split within AEW. Collision became AEW's third major weekly TV show, accompanying Dynamite on Wednesdays and Rampage on Fridays. The birth of Collision meant the death of AEW Dark and Dark: Elevation, the company's weekly YouTube shows that featured upcoming talent from the ever-expanding roster - but even with those two programmes cut from the weekly schedule, AEW was now producing a lot of TV for viewers to get through every week. Would Collision be able to establish its own feel, and somehow make itself must-see programming in an oversaturated market?

Moreover, would the separation of Punk from his enemies within the company be enough to keep the peace? After all, the various parties in the previous year's dispute would still cross paths at pay-per-views and other selected occasions across the year - and in the meantime, Punk in particular was likely to say something sooner or later that would stir the pot. Collision might have been Punk's kingdom for now, but heavy is the head that wears the crown...

CHAPTER 8
COLLISION COURSE: CM PUNK, AEW, AND A COMPANY AT A CROSSROADS

ISSUE 50, SEPTEMBER 2023
JOHN ELLUL

WITH AEW'S *new Saturday show up and running, and CM Punk front and centre, the next few months will be crucial to the company's future.*

Guess who's back? Back again. Philip's back – tell a friend. But maybe not Colt Cabana.

So, here we go again. As promised, a major new weekly AEW show has kicked off with CM Punk addressing the masses at the United Center in front of thousands of rabid Chicagoans. The wrestling world turned up and tuned in to hear what the man himself had to say, following a lengthy period of silence.

Didn't we just do this all a couple of years ago? I don't know about you, but this writer has an unshakeable sense of Déjà vu.

It might feel another lifetime, but 'The First Dance,' CM Punk's glorious AEW debut-turned-homecoming parade took place less than two years ago, in August 2021. In that time, Punk has managed a hero's welcome, several feuds, two world title victories, a pair of injuries, a nine-month hiatus, and, of course, a candid appearance at a post-match media scrum.

To be fair, after seven years out of wrestling, Punk had plenty of lost time to make up for. Perhaps that was on his mind when, on 17 June, he stepped out to open the first ever episode of AEW Collision, the Jacksonville, Florida-based promotion's new weekly Saturday night show on TNT. His eagerly awaited promo touched on a number of things, from alluding to AEW's rumoured new TV contract to, of course, his autumn adversaries. Punk declared:

"Boo me, cheer me, love me, hate me, you all do it because you know I'm right. You can call me whatever you want. You know what [Warner Bros Discovery CEO] David Zasloff calls me? One Bill Phil. That's because I am the one true genuine article in a business full of counterfeit bucks. The king is back, baby, and I do have a lot of things to get off my chest."

Ratings-wise, the first episode of Collision averaged 816,000 viewers on TNT – more than the aforementioned debut of AEW Rampage. With a 0.33 rating in the important 18-49 demo, it also topped the preceding edition of AEW's flagship programme, Dynamite, in that metric.

The new show – and Punk's role in it – has been well received, from a commercial and critical point of view. From those in the arena, that was inevitable given's Punk's status as a hometown hero. The immediate reaction from the pro wrestling commentariat has been slightly more guarded, as you might expect given Punk's track record for self-implosion, but people seem cautiously optimistic.

Writing the day after the show aired, Wrestling Observer Newsletter editor Dave Meltzer noted:

"I expected a good number with the debut of a new show that has been promoted for a month and C.M. Punk's return being heavily promoted as well. It's more about the staying power past the novelty but all indications I had was interest in this show was high.

The need for consistency was also true about AEW Rampage. Many years ago it was a similar story for the first episode of WCW Thunder. New wrestling shows launched to great fanfare by popular companies during hot periods for the business tend to do be an instant success. A sudden flop would be an outlier in this case.

REMEMBER RAMPAGE?

For all its reliance on nostalgia, AEW boss Tony Khan does not have to study the failings of World Championship Wrestling for an example of what can happen when a wrestling company overreacts to a sustained period of success. In 2021, TNT's reaction to how brilliantly Dynamite had performed was to offer Khan a further hour of prime-time television. There is a pretty easy logic to see why the Fulham Football Club executive agreed.

For all the concern that people have expressed that AEW should be careful not to overstretch itself, things are not that simple. Whether running a wrestling company or producing a television show (or both), it is not a foregone conclusion that these ventures will be popular. And it certainly should not be taken for granted that your television partners will get in touch to tell you that things are going so well, they want to offer you an additional timeslot.

What is Khan supposed to do – turn it down? To say 'No thanks' to the extra advertising revenue; to deny himself the opportunity to grow AEW's name even further; or to decline the chance at quality television time for many of the talents on his stacked roster? We would all be questioning his sanity if he did something like that. It does set him quite the conundrum – damned if they take on more television hours, and damned if they don't.

There are a few practical issues at hand which will gain some clarity in the coming months. One of those is what will become of AEW Rampage. The show received a significant build up as the number-two show and has now in less than two years been relegated to an afterthought. In isolation it is not hard to see why.

Rampage famously debuted to more than a million viewers which represented an incredible success which AEW was, and should remain, very proud of. A large number of fans had craved CM Punk's return, and those that didn't were still curious to hear what he had to say. No one expected that level of interest or excitement every week – but what followed was particularly disappointing.

Match quality declined and a pattern emerged with name stars often in uncompetitive match-ups, and often with little or no build, or much storyline input. Khan acknowledged the complaints in a media scrum in December of last year and, as he tends to do, made some big promises. He said:

"I think now is a time for me to really put all hands on deck to put the strongest shows I can on Friday, and I always try to listen to the feedback from the fans, so going forward I'm going to try to put things on the Friday show that I think will have the best chance to bring in that audience, so I'll look back at what has historically done really well because we've had a lot of good history of shows that have done well on Friday."

We now know of course that Khan's actual plan was to create a new second show for AEW and relegate Rampage even lower down the food chain. That's fine – as long as Collision does not repeat the same pattern. That will be incredibly difficult to avoid, for a number of reasons.

Firstly, there is the Saturday night slot. Assuming that has not been picked for sentimental reasons (it won't be starting at 6.05pm, after all), Saturday may historically be a TV wrestling night but it has not been for years. Khan must realise that this will be a tall order to get people to stay in on a Saturday night – and in the wrestling market, it will regularly be up against WWE shows these days.

Then, there is the much bigger issue with what – and who – will actually take place on Collision on a weekly basis. This, at its core, is what pulled Rampage asunder so swiftly. Punk is established as the number one name on this side of the roster – that makes sense. But who else is there? We can make a good guess that Samoa Joe, Miro, and Andrade will comprise the top-tier for the show, but can those names – especially the latter two – truly make a difference.

And if AEW had the ability to write and execute two coherent, weekly narratives – why did it not already do that with Rampage? For even the biggest AEW supporters, these are definitely questions worth asking.

A TRIUMPH FOR THE AGES

All Elite Wrestling has been - and continues to be – a success of historic proportions. Since its inception in January 2019, the company has produced a compelling weekly television product, an impressive roster, a robust regular pay-per-view schedule, a live event business, and much more. Perhaps most importantly, AEW has harnessed the wave of popularity that wrestling is experiencing, and the passion of the fandom, to develop a fiercely loyal following.

There are plenty of counterarguments you can make. Such as the fact that this would not have been possible if not for the deep pockets of Shahid Khan; the idea that this would not have happened if WWE had not already defined the modern wrestling sandpit for AEW to play in; or the notion that AEW has plenty of negatives it needs to work out.

There is substance in each of those viewpoints – but even those discussions, be they motivated by misplaced tribalism or not, must acknowledge how well AEW has done, and how quickly. Even if the company closed its doors tomorrow, it has created history that is will be difficult – if not impossible – for any other start-up wrestling company to emulate.

Sure, it's not beyond the realms of possibility that a billionaire may want to compete with WWE in future. It's pretty obvious that there is appetite for competition. And sure, that billionaire may have experience running other sports franchises. But the Khans had more than that. In Tony, they had someone with a keen sense of what a section of the wrestling audience values. Combine that with the moment in time that was the wrestling scene of the mid-2010s.

AEW's most recent success of course has been the incredible number of tickets sold for the company's debut UK show, at Wembley Stadium. Breaking the news in May on Twitter, Khan announced:

"Thanks to amazing support from our fans, AEW All In London at Wembley Stadium has sold 60,000 tickets for £6.1M ($7.7M)! This is one of the greatest success stories in wrestling history!"

Plenty of people have acknowledged this incredible success story for what it is. However, you cut it, it's a fantastic number, and one that will surely rise before the day arrives. The likelihood is All In London will be have an attendance that puts in within the top 20 shows ever promoted by a US wrestling company. Not bad for a group that did not exist five years ago.

AEW Executive Vice Presidents Matt and Nick Jackson certainly think so. The Young Bucks could be forgiven for thinking that history is repeating itself, triumph as they did in putting on the original All In back in 2018. Piece of cake this promoting game, eh?

SUCCESS BREEDS SUCCESS?

AEW is not on the hot streak it first blazed from 2019, that much is certainly true. The wave of support which helped sustain it through the first year and tough early months of the pandemic has long dissipated, and the promotion needs to figure out the next several months and come out of it better.

From creative to pay-per-view buy-rates to television ratings, each of those has dipped. Anyone who assumed that things would always be brilliant was short-sighted to say the least. Equally, adding more 'things' does not necessarily mean all is rosy. ECW, don't forget, had its own computer games, action figures, magazine, and such.

In a pragmatic sense, the fact that the company is still operating successfully and stably, is a good thing in itself. There are no urgent causes for concerns, such as the impending loss of a television deal. On the contrary, AEW's partners love what it is doing and are pushing for it to keep doing it – see 'AEW All Access' as evidence of that. The long-awaited AEW video game is finally here.

Pay-per-view buy rates are very respectable – but also not what they were. March's Revolution pulled in an estimated 130,000 buys, down a little from November's Full Gear, but significantly from the previous year's Revolution, which drew between 165,000 and 173,000.

Perhaps this is a hint that the addition of Rampage to the schedule gave AEW's metrics an initial shot in the arm before tailing off – maybe this will happen with Collision. Maybe it's part of the long-term strategy to have a new buzzy show every two years. Ticket sales, though, have been sluggish for Collision, even despite the plan to pitch up in traditional wrestling hotbeds such as Toronto, Calgary and the Greens-boro Coliseum.

Forbidden Door 2 had AEW loyalists salivating, showing

that Khan does retain the ability to give his core audience what they want. But will that be enough? History suggests not.

The Wembley attendance is the kind of tremendous number that even naysayers have to recognise. Long-time AEW detractor Eric Bischoff even made positive noises, albeit caveated ones. Speaking on his 83 Weeks podcast in May he said:

"I wasn't surprised at the success. I knew they were gonna do well. I said that as soon as it was announced, that I knew they were gonna do extremely well. It's an unmitigated success. There's no way you can spin it, twist it, turn it any other way. It's a huge, huge accomplishment."

Bischoff was quick to point out that the number does not seem to correlate with other metrics for AEW, such as television ratings, which have proven pretty stagnant for the past several months. As Senior Vice President of WCW, the biggest attendance Bischoff ever presided over was the 41,412 who packed into the Georgia Dome in July 1998.

As unlikely as it seemed from the crowd reaction that night, like much of the story of World Championship Wrestling, Bill Goldberg's big win over Hollywood Hogan turned out to be another step on the path to the company's eventual demise. Bischoff talks a good game, but he certainly knows a thing or two about taking on WWE. WCW provided plenty of examples about how it could be done – and what not to do.

A WARNING FROM HISTORY

Days before the first episode of AEW Collision, Tony Khan was in full promotional mode. Detailing the thought process behind launching additional television exposure, Khan noted *new show, which we eventually called Thunder, was supposed to be another two-hour live event broadcast every week in prime time.*

"I thought to myself, My God, we're already operating at 110 percent capacity. This has to be a joke."

Sadly for WCW and its fans, the additional request – or demand – was no joke. Though some would stay Thunder, and WCW, quickly became a laughing stock.

THUNDERSTRUCK

WCW Thunder took to the airwaves on 8 January 1998, and while the initial ratings were great, these quickly tailed off. Sound familiar? As the months passed it quickly became clear that what WCW had achieved was not to duplicate its intensely popular flagship show, but to dilute it. Thunder was a clear and obvious demonstration of a company overstretching its limits, and should be remembered as a key example of the company's gluttony.

The first episode encapsulated both WCW's success and problems succinctly. The show was an ill-advised two hours long, and featured 11 matches, but actual in-ring action only amounted for a little over half an hour. Plenty of time for skits and interviews, which has been par for the course from this era onwards. Perhaps more startling is the roster that performed on the night.

Randy Savage, Ric Flair, Scott Hall, Kevin Nash, Goldberg, Lex Luger, Dallas Page and The Giant all wrestled, while Hulk Hogan and Bret Hart – signed from the WWF specifically to be the star of this particular show – also appeared. No wonder Bischoff was eventually convinced to put aside his fears over watering down the product when he had that many names to accommodate.

There are certainly shades of AEW in terms of roster size

that it was the will of the network – as if that somehow makes it inevitable. He told Sports Illustrated:

"We have an amazing opportunity with AEW on Saturday nights on TNT, starting June 17, and it was truly the brainchild of [Warner Bros Discovery president] David Zaslav. He asked about more AEW, specifically Saturday nights, on TNT. When it was pitched to us by TNT, I was so excited. It's so exciting the timing [of CM Punk's return from injury] coincides with the launch of Collision."

Yep, funny how that worked out isn't it? We may never get any official word on what, if any, suspension CM Punk received for his part in the All Out post-event media scrum, but it is true that he needed several months to rehab his left triceps, torn during his match with Jon Moxley that evening. Clearly, when the option of a new show came into view, the temptation to coordinate Punk's return with the launch was too much to resist.

It was a similar story for a certain podcaster when he found himself in the same situation more than 25 years ago. WCW experienced the hottest year in company history in 1997, thanks to the rise of the New World Order and the must-watch nature of Monday Nitro, doing the unthinkable by consistently beating WWF to become, for a time, the number one wrestling company in the world.

That was just the start of WCW's problems, as Eric Bischoff described in his 2006 autobiography, Controversy Creates Cash. As he told it, the moment he found out that Turner network executives, thrilled by WCW's performance, wanted more brought him an undeniable sinking feeling. He wrote:

"I got a phone call from [Turner Sports President] Harvey Schiller. "By the way," he added. "I just got out of a meeting with Ted [Turner, TBS & TNT founder]. Because of the success of Monday Nitro on TNT, Ted wants to launch a show on TBS."

"It took him several minutes to convince me he was serious. The

The roster bloat is perhaps another symptom of AEW's relationship to WWE. Much as WCW did in the 1990s, and TNA in the 2000s and 2010s, Tony Khan's brainchild exists as a reaction to WWE, when it comes to talent, and who they can and can't sign. The truth is, as soon as anyone with any name value (and several others with none) at all leaves WWE, they inevitably pop up in AEW – whether the company actually needs them or not.

A perpetual problem is created from having too many people signed to your roster. A promoter needs lots of great talent for the shows to be exciting; the promoter signs everyone they can; the promoter has too much talent to fit on the show; the promoter needs another show; the promoter needs more talent; and repeat.

What is even more baffling is that a company can have so many performers yet so few main eventers. And that is where CM Punk comes in. Even after a lengthy absence, the company is dependent on his waning star power, and everyone knows it.

All the signs from the first show point towards an effort to change that, which is exactly what AEW need, and fans should welcome this. Career mid-carders like Andrade and Miro have resisted the temptation to return to WWE and now its time for Tony Khan to let them, and others, show what they can do. They, in turn, need to repay the faith that Khan has shown in them. Their showing on the first Collision, where both returned with victories after their respective hiatuses was a good start.

A lack of marquee talent is one of the things that will kill a company over the long-term. It impacts ratings, sponsorships, licensing deals, house show attendances, pay-per-view buys, and more. AEW has survived, and at times thrived, with a thin top line consisting of Punk, Bryan Danielson, Chris Jericho, Kenny Omega, Jon Moxley, MJF, and very little else. For all the derision it has drawn over the years, WWE's insistence on building around a 'face of the company' for each generation has always been focused on the bigger picture.

If you were Tony Khan, and your main event scene looked like that, you would be calling Goldberg and making sure Punk returned too, no matter what other people – or perhaps your own gut instinct – were telling you. Those short-term options come with problems of their own. Fresh faces can fix that, and with the right focus and the right people, a new show could be the breeding ground to develop exactly that.

The inability to concentrate his attention sufficiently in one area is an accusation levelled at Khan constantly. In addition to being CEO, President, and Executive Producer of AEW, he also holds senior executive roles with an NFL franchise, a Premier League football team, and purchased a second wrestling company last year for no obvious reason other than the fact it was available.

He - and AEW – are swamped. Knee-deep in 'stuff.' Over the last six months alone, in addition to Collision, AEW has done the following: announced a huge London show; staged the second Forbidden Door crossover with NJPW; expanded its house show slate; aired a reality show; continued discussions for a streaming service and a new TV deal; rebranded one of its title belts; launched its first video game; kicked off the second Owen Hart Cup; and continued with the talent signings, ROH tapings, Dynamite, pay-per-views, and more.

Oh, and the Khans may also want – or wanted at some point in the past – to buy Bellator. And WWE, when it was for sale. Who knows? They say if you stand still you move backwards. What does it mean if you try and run in several directions at once?

On 17 June at least, AEW pitched things perfectly and gave itself a brilliant platform to succeed with an engaging first episode of Collision. It will need more than that. One man it has to thank for the good showing, like it or not, was CM Punk. Still one of the greatest wrestling promos ever, he had plenty to say. Whether this all ends in a money-making programme with the Bucks and Omega remains to be seen, but his kiss-off was pretty ominous:

"And there are those of you who, I'm sure, were praying to whatever God you believe in that I'm going to walk into the sunset, never to be seen again. But until there is somebody in this company that can fill these boots, they belong on my feet."

Tell him when he's telling lies? Don't worry Phil – we will.

RULE OF ENGAGEMENT #19: ACT SWIFTLY AT THE FIRST HINT OF MUTINY

Upon his return to AEW as the main focal point for Collision, CM Punk wasted no time in reasserting his presence. His first appearance on the new show was met with a thunderous response from fans, signaling their eagerness to welcome him back into the fold. Punk's charisma and mic skills, key elements of his persona, were on full display as he engaged in intense promos that reignited long-standing rivalries and sparked new ones. In the ring, Punk delivered performances against the likes of Samoa Joe and Ricky Starks that reminded fans of his technical prowess and storytelling ability.

Then, a month away from the company's big night at Wembley Stadium, Punk started referring to himself as the 'Real World's Champion' because he had never lost the title prior to his suspension - it was a good hook for his character, with plenty of promise for an eventual showdown with whoever was the officially recognised world champion later down the line - assuming that he lasted that long in the company, of course.

As it turned out, to make such an assumption would have been a mistake. By the time a record London crowd assembled at Wembley for 'All In', Punk was on the brink of yet another controversy that would cast a shadow over one of the promotion's biggest ever nights. Given the events of the previous autumn, perhaps this wasn't a surprise - lightning was about to strike twice, and this time the storm that followed would cause more damage than ever.

CHAPTER 9
STRAIGHT EDGE, HIGH STAKES: A LOOK BACK AT CM PUNK'S TIME IN AEW

ISSUE 49, OCTOBER 2023
CONNEL RUMSEY AND DEE ADAMS

CONNEL RUMSEY *and Dee Adams take a look at CM Punk's eventful stint in All Elite Wrestling.*

For the longest time, wrestling fans around the world could've been forgiven for thinking they'd seen the last of CM Punk. 'The Voice of the Voiceless' made his final appearance in a squared circle at the 2014 Royal Rumble where he entered at number 1 before lasting 49 minutes to make it to the final 4. Despite his impressive Rumble showing, Punk was not mentioned the next night on Raw, nor did he appear on that week's episode of SmackDown, for which he was advertised. Word quickly began to spread that Punk had walked out of the company but Vince McMahon was quick to reassure investors that he was simply 'taking a sabbatical'. In the months that followed, the wrestling world buzzed with speculation as to what CM Punk's WWE status was. Was he injured? Had he really turned his back on the WWE? Would wrestling fans see him again? By the time WWE announced they had parted ways with CM Punk on 2nd June 2014, the news wasn't all that surprising. Still, wrestling fans were massively disappointed to hear that Punk was gone, especially as it felt that he still had so much to achieve within the industry.

At 35 years of age, CM Punk was officially retired but that didn't mean he was ready to slow down. He decided to use his newfound freedom to pursue other things. He began writing for Marvel comics, making his debut with a story in *Thor Annual #1*. He also co-wrote a Drax the Destroyer series with well-known comic book writer Cullen Bunn. He also set his sights on the UFC, signing a contract with them in December 2014. Punk wasn't able to recreate his professional wrestling success inside the octagon. He suffered a first round submission loss in his debut match and didn't fare much better in his second. His stint in the UFC was short but memorable, and in typical Punk fashion, divisive. While some praised his courage to step out of his comfort zone and try something drastically different, others criticised the UFC for signing him purely based on his fame rather than his fighting skills. His MMA record stands at 0-2.

Throughout Punk's post-WWE years, questions about a potential wrestling return lingered. He remained adamant that he would never return to the WWE citing health reasons and creative differences. At the time, the WWE was the only sizeable wrestling promotion in North America and it looked increasingly unlikely that fans would ever see Punk inside the squared circle again. All that changed in 2019 with the creation of Tony Khan's AEW. The promotion quickly gained attention in the wrestling world for its intent to provide an alternative to mainstream wrestling, with a focus on an athlete-centred, fan-first approach to the sport. Would this be enough to lure Punk out of retirement?

Rumours began to swirl that discussions were taking place between Punk and Khan, and for the first time since the 2014 Royal Rumble, seeing Punk inside a wrestling ring seemed a lot more than a pipe dream. Excitement reached a fever pitch in the summer of 2021 when AEW booked the

United Center in Punk's hometown of Chicago for the second episode of their new Rampage show, a show titled 'The First Dance'.

THE RETURN

On the 20th August 2021, it finally happened. 'Cult of Personality' hit and a sold out United Centre erupted. A genuinely emotional looking CM Punk walked down the ramp, pausing multiple times to soak in the atmosphere, and what an atmosphere it was. It was a true hero's welcome, with all of Chicago on their feet to embrace their hometown boy. When he finally got to the ring, Punk appealed to the passionate crowd, explaining that he'd heard them during the past 7 years, but he was never going to improve physically, mentally, and spiritually in the WWE, the place he claimed made him sick in the first place. He then sat in the middle of the ring, evoking memories of his infamous pipebomb promo and began to recall his final day in Ring of Honor before joining the WWE. "*August 13th 2005 I left professional wrestling. August 20th 2021, I'm back.*" Punk's message was loud and clear - he wasn't just returning to the sport; he was reclaiming a part of his identity that had been lost. This moment wasn't merely a comeback; it was a rebirth.

Punk then shifted his focus to the future, addressing the AEW roster and the opportunities that lay ahead. He expressed his excitement about the young, talented wrestlers in AEW, and his eagerness to work with them, learn from them, and teach them, starting with Darby Allin at the All Out PPV.

Punk's return was perhaps the worst kept secret in modern wrestling history. Still, the wrestling world was ablaze in the days that followed. AEW uploaded the footage of his debut onto YouTube and it had millions of views within hours. Everyone was talking about it. Even fans who had drifted away from wrestling over the years were tuning in to check it out. Punk's reemergence made fans wonder if AEW could be a viable competitor to the WWE after all.

Darby Allin was an interesting choice for Punk's return match. The buildup to their bout at AEW's All Out 2021 was a study in nuanced storytelling. Punk, renowned for his eloquence and psychological acumen, portrayed Allin as a kindred spirit from a different era. One of the 'four pillars' of AEW, Allin is known for being rich in character despite his sparse verbal communication. He represents the evolving face of wrestling. His portrayal as the enigmatic, risk-taking underdog provided a stark contrast to Punk's more grounded, yet equally intense style. The presence of Sting in Allin's corner added a multi-generational depth to the storyline.

The match between CM Punk and Darby Allin at AEW's All Out 2021 was a standout encounter showcasing a blend of experience and innovation. Punk, wrestling for the first time in seven years, brought a methodical, technical style that highlighted his veteran status. His every move was calculated, echoing his past as a top wrestler. Allin, known for his high-risk approach, contrasted sharply with Punk. His fast-paced, daring style added an element of unpredictability to the match—Allin's willingness to take risks made for an exciting dynamic against Punk's more grounded technique.

The match was well-paced, mixing technical wrestling with high-impact moves. Punk's seamless return to form was impressive, while Allin demonstrated he could compete with wrestling's best. The storytelling in the ring was a key element, with Punk's comeback narrative intertwining with Allin's ambition to rise in the ranks.

The climax saw Punk executing his signature GTS (Go To Sleep) for the win. The match's end, though decisive, didn't overshadow Allin's performance; it rather highlighted his potential.

After the match, the mutual respect shown between the two wrestlers capped off the event, symbolising a generational bridge. Punk, it seemed, was deadly serious when he said he wanted to work with, teach, and learn from the younger talent in the AEW locker room.

DANCING WITH THE DEVIL

There was one rivalry that the entire AEW fanbase was waiting for when Punk arrived in the company, and that was with another AEW pillar, the loudmouth Maxwell Jacob Friedman, MJF. Fortunately, they didn't have to wait long.

On the 17th November 2021, MJF came to the ring during an episode of Dynamite and began to verbally eviscerate the crowd in attendance whilst simultaneously self-aggrandising. *"I deserve to be the next AEW World Champion because nobody in that locker room is nearly as good as me. Nobody in that locker room is on my level."* CM Punk's music hit and the 'best in the world' made his way to the ring with an amused smile on his face. The mere sight of the two men standing across from each other in the ring was enough to elicit a "holy sh*t" chant from the crowd in attendance. MJF, in his typical heelish fashion, tried to make nice with Punk, extending out his hand and introducing himself. Punk simply laughed and walked away, leaving an enraged and humiliated MJF standing the the middle of the squared circle. The mind games had begun.

Over the next few weeks, the two men would verbally clash in the ring multiple times, cutting a series of promos that cut just a little too close to the bone. It was a masterclass in storytelling, with both Punk and MJF displaying why they're regarded as two of the best to ever pick up a mic.

Their promos were deeply personal, scathing, and often blurred the lines between character and reality. They touched on various subjects from each other's careers, personal lives, and wrestling philosophies, captivating the audience with their intensity and authenticity. The pair's rivalry took the fans on an emotional rollercoaster, with MJF manipulating the crowd into taking his side over Punk's before the wolf shed its sheep's clothing, and 'The Devil' we know today was born.

Both online and inside the ring, MJF had been mocked for his previous love of CM Punk, with a photo of the young villain beaming next to Punk at a meet and greet some years earlier becoming a source of much amusement. Punk even alluded to the photo himself, saying that for him meeting the young Maxwell Jacob Friedman had just been 'another Friday'. The next week on Dynamite, a visibly upset MJF came to the ring and began to appeal to the audience's empathetic side, stating that for him, it wasn't just another Friday, it was everything, and at times in his life professional wrestling was the only thing that got him out of bed in the morning. He began to talk about the difficulties he faced as a child due to his litany of learning disabilities. He talked about being bullied by his peers and how the only thing that cheered him up was the idea of meeting his hero, CM Punk, at an autograph signing. He made a promise to himself that he was going to grow strong, that he was going to become a professional wrestler just like CM Punk. His sadness turned to anger and hurt when he spoke of feeling neglected after Punk turned his back on the industry and how the disappointment made him give up on his dreams for several years until he decided he was going to become 'the best in the world' in spite of CM Punk. Now tearful, MJF looked into the camera and called CM Punk a gutless coward for leaving behind those who needed him the most. A shaken Punk made his way to the ring and asked MJF if his story was true. With a nod of confirmation, MJF left his former idol looking guilt-stricken in the middle of the ring, with the lines between good and evil suddenly feeling very blurred. As fans, we now understood what compelled MJF to behave to way he did, and many related to him. MJF was no longer just a brash cocky heel, he was the consequence of Punk's actions, what happened when the voiceless were left without a voice.

The two men faced each other three times during their feud, with MJF coming out on top during their first two clashes. Their final encounter took place at the Revolution PPV in March 2022 in a dog collar match. The choice of stipulation was interesting as it drew immediate parallels to CM Punk's legendary feud with Raven in early 2000s Ring of Honor which featured a famously bloody and brutal dog collar match. Acknowledging this, on the night of the Revolution PPV, CM Punk came to the ring to his old ROH entrance music, Miseria Cantare, while wearing his old ROH ring gear. The match itself felt deeply personal. It was a violent affair and the two men beat each other to bloody pulps. In the end it was CM Punk who was victorious after he hit MJF with his signature G2S (Go to Sleep) move and then followed it up by hitting the younger wrestler in the face with his own Dynamite Ring. The iconic bout is considered among the very best in the history of both the stipulation and the promotion of All Elite Wrestling.

WORKERS RIGHTS

Looking back, Revolution really marked the end of Punk's honeymoon period in AEW, as he would soon take aim at the AEW World Championship, held by then-champion 'Hangman' Adam Page.

As far as feuds go, CM Punk and Adam Page's rivalry was gearing up to be lukewarm at best, especially when compared to Punk's earlier feud with MJF, and even his mini-feud with Eddie Kingston. Beyond the fact that Punk was challenging for the AEW World Championship at the Double or Nothing PPV, there was very little to get excited about. The two men cut promos on each other during the Dynamite before the PPV. Again, it seemed like a relatively innocuous segment. Little did fans know that it was the spark that would lead to something much bigger. During his promo, Page went off-script and said, *"You talk a big game about workers' rights. Well, you've shown the complete opposite since you got here. I love this place, I care about this place. This is my home. And this Sunday at Double or Nothing, I will not be defending this championship against you. No, for the first time in my life, I'll be defending All Elite Wrestling from you."* Although slightly confusing and irrelevant, Page's 'workers' rights' comment didn't seem that bad, especially considering some of the extremely personal jabs MJF had made in the previous months. However, Punk really took exception to it, and to fully understand why we need to go back in time to the year 1999, at the Steel Domain Wrestling School in St Paul, Minnesota...

Way before he was CM Punk, Phil Brooks was a young man who dreamed of becoming a professional wrestler. He began training at Ace Steel's wrestling school and it was here that he met another aspiring wrestler named Scott Colton, better known to most as Colt Cabana. The two young men became fast friends as they travelled and worked together across the mid-west independent scene before both being signed to ROH in 2002. They quickly rose to prominence within the promotion, forming the Second City Saints and going on to feud with the likes of Raven and Generation Next. In a 2007 interview with wrestlinginc.com, Cabana said of their friendship, *"Punk and I have been a team since basically the first month I was training. We travelled the roads together for a very long time. He's my brother in wrestling and life. I talk to him every day."*

In 2005 CM Punk signed to WWE and in 2007 Colt Cabana followed in his footsteps. Though Punk's WWE career was considerably more successful (Cabana was rebranded as Scotty Colton before being released in 2009) the two men remained close, with Cabana even getting a shoutout during the infamous pipebomb promo. In 2014, after being released from WWE, CM Punk appeared on Cabana's popular *Art of Wrestling* podcast and held nothing back going into detail about the creative and professional frustrations he felt during his time in the company. Most noteworthily, Punk accused WWE and one of its doctors, Chris Amann, of negligence. He said the company ignored a methicillin-resistant Staphylococcus aureus (MRSA) infection, which ended up being life-threatening after WWE doctors loaded him up with Z-PAK and sent him out to wrestle, which resulted in him soiling himself during a match on an episode of SmackDown.

WWE and Amann sued both Punk and Cabana for defamation, but Punk won the lawsuit. However, later Cabana would try to sue Punk, claiming that his friend had agreed to cover his legal fees but had reneged on the promise. Punk claimed that Cabana was being greedy and trying to extort him. Cabana tried to sue Punk for $200,000 for the legal fees associated with Cabana hiring his own legal representation arguing that their prior agreement was that Punk would cover all legal costs. He was also seeking $1 million in punitive and exemplary damages. Punk filed a countersuit for $600,000 for general damages along with interest and legal fees associated with the Dr. Amann case that Punk claimed cost him $1.2 million. The two men eventually settled their claims, but their friendship was irrevocably broken.

When Punk signed with AEW in August 2021, Colt Cabana was also working for the company as a member of the Dark Order. After a while, his appearances with the Dark Order stopped and he was eventually moved to the ROH roster. Rumours began to swirl that Punk had demanded that his former best friend be released, rumours that he attributed to The Elite, hence why the 'workers' rights' comment got under his skin. Punk would continue to deny having anything to do with Cabana's transfer to the ROH roster, and would later say at *that* press conference, "*I haven't been friends with this guy since at least 2014, late 2013…I have f*ck all to do with him. I want nothing to do with him. I do not care where he works or where he doesn't work, where he eats, where he sleeps.*"

Whether Punk was indeed responsible for Cabana, the 'workers' rights' comment was enough to fan the flames of animosity between himself, Adam Page, and the other members of The Elite. Despite Punk winning the AEW World Championship, his match with 'Hangman' Adam Page wasn't well received by fans, who found it underwhelming at best. Later Punk would go on to say that he wasn't able to focus on the quality of his performance because he was too preoccupied with making sure Page didn't intentionally injure him during the match. Overall, it was a bad situation and no one came out of it looking good.

BRAWL OUT

A broken foot sustained during an episode of Dynamite would result in Punk being out of action for a number of months. During that time, Jon Moxley defeated Hiroshi Tanahashi to be crown interim AEW World Champion. When Punk made his return in August, he wasted little time confronting the interim champion. Bizarrely, Punk and Moxley's title unification match would not take place at All Out, but rather the August 24 episode of Dynamite, with Moxley squashing Punk in short order.

At All Out, the two men would clash again, this time with Punk taking the victory to be crowned two-time AEW World

Champion. However, during the match he suffered a torn triceps and knew he was going to be out of action for months. After the show, Punk would sit next to a terrified looking Tony Khan at a post-show press conference and launch into a diatribe about AEW's EVPs and 'Hangman' Adam Page, stemming from the rumours he'd believed they were spreading. He referred to The Young Bucks and Kenny Omega as *"irresponsible people who call themselves EVPs and couldn't f*cking manage a Target."* And on Adam Page, he said, *"What did I ever do in this world to deserve an empty-headed f*cking dumbf*ck like 'Hangman' Adam Page to go out on national television and f*cking go into business for himself? For what? What did I ever do? ... Didn't do a goddamn thing."* Punk was angry and he wasn't holding back.

Once the press conference was over, The Young Bucks, Adam Page, and Kenny Omega stormed into Punk's locker room to confront him. Whilst it is not fully known what was said, it's widely believed that the confrontation ended in a multi-man punch up that lasted around six minutes, with Nick Jackson *allegedly* taking a chair to the eye, Punk *allegedly* punching Matt Jackson in the face, and Punk's trainer, Ace Steel, *allegedly* biting Kenny Omega on the arm. Everyone involved in the brawl was suspended, although some, such as Christopher Daniels and Michael Nakazawa had their suspensions lifted when it was revealed they were trying to separate people.

The whole thing was a PR disaster for AEW and did major damage to the public's perception of the company. The incident, which quickly made headlines in the wrestling world, raised serious questions about backstage professionalism and the management of wrestler conduct in AEW. The company had prided itself on being a wrestler-friendly organisation with a strong sense of camaraderie among its talent, but this brawl suggested underlying tensions and issues. Fans and critics alike began to question the company's internal dynamics and the effectiveness of its leadership in managing its stars.

SATURDAY NIGHT'S ALRIGHT

Once the Brawl Out dust had settled, The Elite made their return to AEW in October at the Full Gear. However, with Punk injured, many fans were beginning to speculate whether or not he would return to the company.

On 17th May 2023, AEW and their broadcast partner Warner Bros. Discovery (WBD) announced a third weekly television show titled AEW Collision to air live on TNT as a two-hour show on Saturdays starting June 17, 2023. Punk was almost cleared to wrestle and rumours emerged that he would make his return at the first ever Collison show, which was taking place in his home town of Chicago. These rumours were confirmed in the weeks leading up to the show.

There was still one big black cloud surrounding Punk's return, and that was that no meeting had taken place between him and the Elite, so the issues between the parties were not resolved. However, keeping Punk on Collision and The Elite on Dynamite meant that they could effectively manage the situation by keeping the involved parties separate, at least for the time being. This strategy also allowed AEW to maintain storyline continuity and fan engagement without compromising the quality of their shows. Punk's presence on Collision and the Elite's on Dynamite ensured that both shows had star power and compelling storylines, keeping the audience invested in both programs.

In his return promo, Punk couldn't resist taking shots at the Elite, referring to himself as *"the one true genuine article in a business full of counterfeit bucks."* He also brought out his AEW

World Championship (that he'd been stripped of post-Brawl Out) and said that it was his until someone could pin him or submit him for it.

During that same promo, Punk made another comment alluding to The Elite being 'soft' which prompted a Twitter response from their friend Ryan Nemeth, who claimed Punk was 'the softest man alive'. He was subsequently banned from Collision at the request of Punk, as was AEW's Head of Talent Relations Christopher Daniels, due to Punk hoping to maintain a 'drama free' locker room. Unfortunately, the 'drama free' locker room wouldn't stay 'drama free' for very long.

RUMBLE WITH THE JUNGLE

On 25th August 2023, AEW held their largest ever show, All In, at a sold out Wembley Stadium in London. In the preshow, 'Jungle Boy' Jack Perry wrestled Hook for the FTW Championship. At one point during the match, just as he was about to do a spot on top of a car windshield, Perry looked into the camera and said, "Real glass. Go cry me a river." It was a little bit of a random statement for fans watching at home but a very pointed statement for CM Punk who was watching backstage.

In the weeks prior, Perry had wanted to do a spot involving real glass on an episode of Collision. According to backstage sources, the spot had been approved by the higher ups and was all ready to go. However, when Punk arrived at the arena he vetoed the spot, claiming, "We're not using glass. We don't use glass around here." Punk claimed it was for safety reasons, but Perry believed he was being targeted due to his close friendship with The Young Bucks.

Punk confronted Perry once the latter returned to the

backstage area and according to multiple witnesses things got physical, with Punk shoving, punching, and choking Perry in front of Tony Khan. The Wrestling Observer reported that once things were broken up, Punk allegedly 'lunged' at Khan before telling the AEW boss he would be quitting the company. He then went out and wrestled Samoa Joe in front of more the 70,000 wrestling fans, none of whom knew they were seeing CM Punk in an AEW ring for the final time.

On the 2nd September, Tony Khan released a statement saying that he had to fire CM Punk due to a 'backstage incident' at AEW All In the previous week. "*I've been going to wrestling shows for over 30 years,*" Khan said. "*I've been producing them on this network for nearly four years. Never, in all that time, have I ever felt until last Sunday that my security, my safety, my life was in danger at a wrestling show. I don't think anybody should feel that way at work.*"

And just like that CM Punk was gone, and having burnt bridges with both major North American wrestling promotions the likelihood of seeing him inside the squared circle again seemed doubtful. Then again, this is professional wrestling. If there's one thing fans have learned over the years, it's to never say never...

RULE OF ENGAGEMENT #20: ENLIST THOSE WHO KNOW THE ENEMY BEST

CM Punk's departure from AEW left a vacancy within the company for a major star with name value, but the position didn't stay unfilled for long. Adam 'Edge' Copeland was just finishing up a three-year run with WWE after his memorable return from retirement at Royal Rumble 2020, and was deciding what to do next. His journey in the company he had always called home concluded with one last hoorah on the August 18 episode of SmackDown in his hometown of Toronto - a match against Sheamus, marking the 25th anniversary of his debut with the company.

It was an emotional night that certainly seemed like a farewell, but still many doubted that Copeland would ever go elsewhere. Rumours and discussions about a potential move to AEW began to circulate, fueled by various factors including his reported desire for new challenges and the opportunity to work with a mix of familiar faces and new talents. But when it happened it was still a shock: Copeland debuted in dramatic fashion at the end of the WrestleDream pay-per-view on 1st October 2023 in a moment that captured the attention of the wrestling world, not least because it involved him confronting his ex-tag team partner Christian Cage.

In the post-show press conference, Tony Khan confirmed that Copeland had signed full-time with the company and would make his Dynamite debut on 4th October. On that night he explained that he came to AEW because he saw an opportunity to reunite with Cage one last time and end their careers together as a team. Cage rejected him, sparking the first feud of what may yet prove to be Copeland's final exhilarating run as an in-ring competitor. But whether his arrival in AEW will be a game-changer in the war against WWE remains to be seen.

CHAPTER 10
COPING MECHANISM: WHY AEW NEEDS ADAM COPELAND TO BE A SUCCESS

ISSUE 52, NOVEMBER 2023
JOHN ELLUL

AEW'S *latest big-name acquisition may be the biggest yet. While the former Edge and his millions of fans can look forward to what's to come, Copeland's move is part of a bigger story at play.*

"When I came back out there tonight, I felt free! I felt free and it felt fun! It felt almost like the same feeling I would have when I'd come out for my indie shows back when I was either Adam Impact or Sexton Hardcastle or something. It was this brand new thing that I always wanted to do. That feeling, I felt it out there tonight and that at this stage of my career to feel that, that's special! Come on, 31 years in and to feel that way? That's a gift."

Adam Copeland is All Elite, that much we know. The man of the moment described it as a 'gift' in his first remarks with the company, following his surprise appearance at *WrestleDream*. He may well feel a warm glow of freedom, but you would imagine the cost of signing the multi-time former WWE champion to Tony Khan's deep pockets was probably a fair bit pricier than your average heartfelt offering.

For the "Rated R Superstar," it is easy to understand the sense of liberty he is currently enjoying. Thirteen long, gruelling – and above all incredibly successful years – on WWE's main roster were followed by an injury-enforced retirement of nearly nine years. Then, a career renaissance brought highs the likes of which Copeland must have spent that lost decade wondering if he would ever experience again.

Now, Copeland has a chance for a second rebirth, with a new wrestling employer for the first time in more than a quarter of a century. Coupled with the reaction of the fervent Seattle crowd on his first night, not to mention the fans online (more than 5 million views and counting on AEW's YouTube channel for Copeland's debut), and the original "Mr Money in the Bank" has plenty to be happy about – as do the fans.

From Sting to Billy Gunn, to Jeff Jarrett to Christian Cage, All Elite Wrestling has had tremendous success in harnessing the residual star power of wrestling's ageing patrons, often with focused, sensible – and fun – character-driven arcs. The group will clearly protect and promote Copeland with the same reverence, which will be to the enjoyment of wrestling fans of all stripes.

In isolation, it is the right decision for everyone – for Copeland and his family, the fans, AEW, and WWE. No one should dispute that. But as All Elite Wrestling approaches its fifth anniversary, the company adding ever more older acts to its roster poses a series of questions that go beyond one individual career, and deserve fair scrutiny.

ADAM MAKES AN IMPACT

Copeland is a lifelong wrestling fan and has often shown his respect for the heritage of the sport of kings. In that context it should come as no real surprise that he namechecked two sobriquets he used in his pre-WWE career in his first AEW-endorsed comments: Adam Impact, and Sexton Hardcastle.

Fans have long chortled at the ridiculous Hardcastle moniker for years, an embarrassing open secret of sorts for the WWE Hall of Famer and a sign that, in the early stages of any career, few of us get the chance to mould things exactly how we might like. Less has been said about the 'Adam Impact' name over the years, a title Copeland used in Canadian indies throughout the mid-1990s.

It is a complete coincidence of course that with WWE and AEW a distant second and third, Impact Wrestling is the name of the third biggest wrestling promotion in the United States – though tiny by comparison. There was probably no realistic prospect of Copeland joining Impact in 2023, given the company's limited reach and resources and the presence of AEW. But the existence of the smaller company does bring a parallel.

Simply by virtue of existing without a viable alternative, Impact – as TNA – spent much of its existence as the secondary American promotion behind WWE throughout the noughties and teens. It was during those years, specifically 2005 to 2009, that TNA welcomed a slew of stars who had seen their options in WWE curtailed for a variety of reasons.

In a short space of time, Kevin Nash, Kurt Angle, Booker T, Mick Foley, and – yep, Christian Cage – were just some of the major names who made their way to the lower-level outfit in quick succession. Each had their own reasons, but for all of them it boiled down to the fact that WWE did not want them. With the exception of Christian, who was approaching his prime and being underserved as a mid-carder, the others were career main eventers on a downward trajectory, several of them hampered by injuries or other issues.

In a recent issue of the Wrestling Observer Newsletter, editor and historian Dave Meltzer drew a specific parallel between Adam Copeland joining AEW and Foley's jump to TNA in the 00's. He wrote:

"In some ways it reminds me of Mick Foley going to TNA, which people thought would greatly help the company but numbers really didn't move. Foley was probably more popular at the time than Copeland is now, although Copeland has far more left in the tank when it comes to inside the ring."

There are a few things wrong with this comparison. The subject of popularity is of course a subjective matter, although anyone who saw the reaction to Copeland's 2020 WWE return, or more recent AEW debut may beg to differ. And while Foley was quite a bit younger (44) than the former Edge, who recently turned 50, a mere look at their physiques tells you Copeland has more to contribute than a handful of hardcore and gimmick matches, as was the case with Foley.

The Impact/TNA metaphor bears discussion, nonetheless. During the era of Foley's jump, WWE stars moving to TNA was so commonplace it became a meme before such things really existed in the wider public consciousness. Who would be the next down-on-their-luck WWE-er to burst into the Impact Zone, people wondered, without any sense of fascination. It is a trend TNA became infamous for, but they did not originate it.

For years, AEW has courted WCW comparisons as a way to leverage the potent nostalgia many older fans still harbour. The persistent signing of former WWE stars is one of the elements that built – and then ultimately destroyed – World Championship Wrestling. The competing egos, the spiralling costs, the unrealistic demands, and more, pulled WCW asunder. AEW has avoided such toxicity (with one notable exception). So far.

DAD'S ARMY

AEW has done a decent job of rearing homegrown talent into elevated positions; not least of all, reigning AEW heavyweight champion MJF, as well as Darby Allin and The Acclaimed, to name a few. The company is a patchwork of younger prospects, long-time indie workers, and former WWE talent – pretty much as you would expect. However, there is a delicate balance to be struck, and some notable observations can be drawn.

For one thing, Copeland's decision to jump the fence means the proportion of Attitude Era-stars that now call AEW home, 25 years after the peak of that period for the opposition, is truly staggering. Edge joins Christian, Sting, Chris Jericho, Matt and Jeff Hardy, Billy Gunn, Dustin Rhodes, Jeff Jarrett, Paul Wight, and (non-wrestlers) Jim Ross, and Mark Henry. WWE by comparison employs just one active wrestler from the same time period in Rey Misterio.

Of course, younger does not necessarily mean better, and many of the wrestlers listed above have received plaudits for their performances in their advancing years. The point stands that a very visible disparity has developed between the major performers joining the top two organisations in the wrestling world.

In the same week that Copeland made his debut for AEW, Jade Cargill was given the star treatment in her televised debut for the opposition, greeted by company boss Triple-H in the pre-show to WWE's *Fast Lane*. Seen by many as a future main eventer, Cargill recently turned 31. A few days prior, vignettes ran on NXT for the upcoming debut of Brian Pillman Jr, a year younger than Cargill.

Cody Rhodes remains WWE's biggest get from AEW, and he was 36 when he returned to the Stamford, Connecticut-headquartered company in spring 2022. The message in both directions seems quite clear: Young, up-and-coming prospects unsure if AEW has your best interests at heart? Head on over to WWE for a career of success. Ageing WWE frustrated that bosses won't meet your hefty wage demands? Tony Khan will be happy to!

The picture is more complex than that. AEW signs and promotes plenty of young talent. Nick Wayne, Skye Blue and Julia Hart have all done incredible work in their short careers under the All Elite banner and have an average age of 21. Young talent can certainly prosper in AEW. Then what?

Copeland's comments about being reinvigorated are genuine and heartfelt. Unfortunately, they come at a time when AEW has cooled off greatly in terms of audience appeal, and it does not necessarily seem like signing new stars, no matter how big the name value, is the way to fix the company's myriad problems.

From falling ratings, to diminishing live attendance, to an over-stuffed roster, and too many hours of television, AEW is in danger of becoming a bloated mess, and one man alone cannot fix that.

YOU THINK YOU KNOW ME

For all that Copeland's initial comments about his move to AEW sound like a ringing endorsement of the upstart company, there is plenty to interpret if you dig a little deeper. Khan may not have been delighted to hear his newest signing describe the buzz he got from the crowd as similar to "indie shows" he used to work three decades ago.

Clearly, the former Edge was drawing a parallel to the raw energy of the crowd – but with AEW's live show numbers struggling as they are, it was perhaps a misplaced thought. While we're in the mood for nitpicking, there was also the claim from the "Rated R Superstar" that this was something he'd "always wanted to do."

Copeland had the opportunity to be All Elite from almost day one and passed the opportunity up. It has been widely reported Khan approached Copeland in the summer of 2019 with the intention of having him debut as a marquee signing on the first ever episode of *Dynamite* – a spot originally given, underwhelmingly, to the former Jack Swagger.

To be fair to the Ontario native, AEW was a fledgling operation at that point with no guarantee of the success that was in the company's immediate future. No one could blame him for taking the safer route of returning to WWE, the company which made him. Given how Vince McMahon and company positioned Edge upon his 2020 return, it was the right choice, and Copeland saw his legacy enhanced significantly thanks to WWE.

The former Brood member is not the only one to share thoughts on the move at a post-show press conference in October. Paul Levesque, head of creative for WWE, was asked for his thoughts on Copeland's departure and subsequent AEW debut. As you might expect, the Chief Content Officer was fulsome in his praise for a man who gave his blood, sweat and tears for the WWE cause for decades. After Fast Lane, the man also known as Triple-H commented:

"Time was right for him, time was right for us. I think he had an amazing career and an amazing sendoff here. And I think he felt like he had done what there was to do. We sort of felt, 'Yeah, think you're right.'

"And I wish him the best. I think he said it the other day, there's no animosity here, there's no hard feelings. He's doing what's right for him and his family and I'm happy for him. Very, very happy for him."

Again, it is a beautiful sentiment, and in a snapshot shows the maturity and transparency that Levesque can operate with, surely a good sign for WWE and wrestling as a whole going forward. The truly instructive lesson comes not in hearing Levesque's paternalistic feeling towards the former Edge, but in the way he describes WWE's reaction to Copeland signalling his departure.

Surely there was haggling, some financial back-and-forth. Eventually though, when the moment (presumably) came for Levesque and McMahon to meet a certain figure or watch a company legend walk, they took the latter option. Levesque added, ominously:

"The machine doesn't stop for anyone."

DREAM COME TRUE

Adam Copeland never needed the machine to stop for him at any point in his career. A wrestling fan from his earliest years, he was determined to become a professional wrestler and with skill, determination, and bloody-mindedness, he made it happen to a degree he probably never thought possible.

It is well documented that a young Copeland was in the crowd for WrestleMania VI, alongside lifelong best buddy Jay "Christian" Reso. A fleeting glimpse of the pair can be seen on the broadcast, a magnificently mullet-ed young Copeland sporting a Hulk Hogan t-shirt while watching the Immortal One battled the Ultimate Warrior in the main event. In 2006, Edge recalled:

"Being at Wrestlemania 6, I remember being completely in shock and dumbfounded when Hulk Hogan missed the leg drop and Warrior hit the splash and got the 1-2-3. I was devastated."

Within ten years, both Copeland and Reso would be full-fledged WWE stars, teaming together, and living their dreams – as well as appearing on the final WrestleMania of the decade, helping the Undertaker to 'hang' the Big Boss Man.

In hindsight it might be tempting to think that Copeland's

path from super fan to WWE legend was predestined, but that would be revisionist given the years of hard work and uncertainty that followed his debut in 1992 at the age of 19. Five years of grinding followed, including a couple of appearances as WCW TV jobber, before the young man received a WWF developmental contract, something which was nowhere near as commonplace as it is today.

The Federation introduced developmental deals sometime in the mid-1990s, with Dwayne Johnson the first significant recipient of such a contract a year prior to Copeland (alongside other lesser lights such as Bart Sawyer and Bull Buchanan). It was around this time that Fed fans got their first real glimpse of Copeland in a WWF Magazine feature which spotlighted a batch of up-and-comers, including the future Edge, Val Venis, Droz, and others.

Edge debuted on television in June 1998 and made an instant impression. By the summer, he was wrestling on pay-per-view, scoring a major victory alongside the red-hot Sable at *SummerSlam*. Throughout the lengthy and prosperous career that followed, it was assumed by most that Edge was a WWE-lifer, having stuck with the company throughout – albeit for the vast majority of this period, there was no viable alternative until AEW arrived.

Another label suits Copeland's place in Vince McMahon's sandpit – that of an outlier. While the mid-1990s recruitment drive started with the (soon-to-be) genre-defining Rocky Maivia, Copeland trailed that by a couple of years. When a slew of WCW refugees arrived in 1999-2000, Edge was already on board. And when the vaunted 'OVW Four' came crashing in a few years later, Copeland was well-established – but separate.

Edge's contemporaries from his entry period into Federation lore are the lesser-spotted class of 1998, if you will. Christian and The Hardy Boyz, of course, are still going in AEW. Elsewhere it was a more forgettable set, comprised of Tiger

Ali Singh, Glenn Kulka, Shawn Stasiak, and a handful of others who made little to no impression.

As part of The Brood, Copeland and Reso caught people's imaginations, a status which was enhanced by their subsequent association with the 'Taker as part of his Ministry of Darkness. It is notable of course that much of Edge's early success came alongside Christian, something that continued as the pair formed a hilarious alliance with Kurt Angle, and then split and developed into solo stars.

Since the time they debuted there has never been any real question about who the bigger star was. Measured purely in accolades, Cage, while no slouch, is a distant second to Copeland. As well as a two-time Royal Rumble winner, 11-time world champion, and former King of the Ring, Edge won a myriad of other titles to put his former partner in the shade.

That was then. Today, with Cage doing some of the best work of his career and experiencing a resurgence of his own, the gap between the two is closer than it has ever been.

FANCY SEEING YOU HERE

Adam Copeland was not the only person who had plenty to say at the post-*WrestleDream* press conference. Cage, who has been giving scintillating work as a despicable heel for years now, was on fine form. Only partially in character, he verbalised what a lot of people have come to think when it comes to the 'other half' of Edge and Christian. He said:

"A few short months ago, people were saying [the AEW TNT] title meant nothing. I've taken it and main evented WrestleDream tonight. I made this title.

"This title, in my opinion, is more prestigious than the world title, mainly because I carry it. But I think my track record speaks

for itself, and I think you have to give me my flowers now, do you not?"

It is a good point, and not mere run-of-the-mill bragging from a wrestling bad guy. The careers of Edge and Christian have run along similar lines since they both debuted within a few months of each other in the WWF, right down to their retirements – with Christian himself required to pause his career due to concussions back in 2014.

Adam Copeland's journey has once again found itself intersected with that of his real-life best friend, and the pair are now reunited at a time when Reso is on an incredible run – perhaps the best of his own long career.

A solid mid-card run was what most expected when Cage joined AEW as another relatively big name signing in the spring of 2021, in a similar category perhaps to Mark Henry and Paul Wight – albeit significantly more mobile than either. After a while building the foundations for what his character would come, Christian Cage turned heel on Jungle Boy and has been on fire ever since.

Cage's "Your father is dead" speech was chilling and quickly became one of the most memorable deliveries in recent wrestling history when his manipulation of Jack Perry became clear. His similarly sinister control over Luchasaurus has been engaging, and now Nick Wayne has been brought under the spell of Cage, who has even wormed his way into holding AEW's secondary singles title.

More and more people are waking up to the fact that Christian is on the best run of his career, and one that could quite conceivably see him move into AEW's main event picture. He is correct in his assessment of how he has elevated the TNT title – even when he was only physically holding it on behalf of Luchasaurus – and he could be a particularly interesting opponent for MJF's world title (even if Mr Friedman senior is very much alive).

Nevertheless, despite holding versions of the world title

on seven occasions across WWE and Impact Wrestling, and multiple tag and singles straps, Christian never quite seemed Edge's equal. Maybe that perception is finally changing, and if so, "Captain Charisma" deserves all the credit in the world for making such a breakthrough after this long in the business.

All of this is to say, it creates an interesting dynamic for Copeland's arrival in Jacksonville. The obvious move of inserting the former Edge into his old tag partner's business was employed immediately, leading to another classic line from Cage when Copeland suggested a reunion a few nights later.

It truly is a stroke of luck for Copeland that Cage is prospering so magnificently in AEW at just the moment he arrives. It is brilliant news for the former WWE Champion, and creates a clear entry point. But what about Christian?

Plenty has been spoken already about how the presence of Christian presents a ready-made, top-line feud for his old colleague, which is great for Adam Copeland. Copeland himself has described how he was encouraged to take the AEW option by his own daughters who wanted to see him work one more time with "Uncle Jay." It is very heartwarming. But for Christian Cage, the timing could not be worse.

Finally, after years in Edge's shadow, he has carved out something for himself. Something interesting and intriguing, a menacing father figure who can destroy a person from within, if he picks the perfect vulnerable victim. What happens to that in a feud with Copeland? A feud, many will recall, WWE already served up years ago.

Plenty of water has passed under the bridge since then of course, but the truth is that Cage does not need Copeland from a narrative point of view. In fact, he's been doing brilliantly well without him. Cage's character will need to pivot somewhat against a man his own age, given that his recent success has been from picking on people younger than him.

It would be easy to assume we have seen everything Edge and Christian have to offer, but they were never going to be kept apart for long if both worked for the same company. Perhaps with the new dimensions Cage is now working with, Copeland will benefit and find his own new space to operate in that he seems to be keen to identify.

If handled correctly, both can prosper.

THE FINAL CHAPTER

Adam Copeland's story has been one of triumphing over adversity. From humble upbringings, to fulfilling his childhood dream, to establishing himself as a superstar when most others fell by the wayside. In 2011, it seemed like the final chapter in his narrative had prematurely been written.

His surprise return to WWE at the 2020 Royal Rumble received a rapturous reaction – surprise returns usually do – and Copeland spent the next two and a half years proving that he still had plenty to offer. The unexpected Edge redux cheered a lot of people up during wrestling's Covid period, as people were legitimately delighted to see the Canadian grappler get the all clear after years of neck trouble.

WWE's treatment of Copeland in the modern era proved that the company respected Edge's significance. In what turned out to be a relatively brief return, comprised of about two-dozen matches, Edge managed a (second) Royal Rumble victory, a WrestleMania main event, and three other Mania matches – all victories, against top talents in the shape of Randy Orton, AJ Styles and Finn Balor.

But the signs were plain to see in Copeland's final months with WWE that the company did not know what to do with him and had, maybe, outgrown him. Copeland himself told CBS Sports in a recent interview as much:

"I kind of got the sense there wasn't really a plan [in WWE]. I get it because what else do we do? What else is there to do? And after 25 years I've literally done everything there. So, what do we do? It wasn't anybody's fault. I was coming up against creative walls too. I was having a hard time coming up with ideas and that's not usually the case. I think they were too."

The hope must be, then, that AEW has a clear plan, and engaging creative, for Copeland, or he runs the risk of being unwittingly positioned once more as a nostalgia act popping in for a brief visit. Having a whole roster of new programmes to go through should help. A few old foes to return to, and a plethora of new faces to help elevate.

Copeland, who recently turned 50, should thrive. For AEW to do the same, the focus needs to be on utilising the WWE Hall of Famer's remaining years for the benefit of those who can carry the company for the next ten years and beyond. It will take nuance and careful planning, but pulling it off and breathing new life into AEW could be one of Adam Copeland's crowning achievements.

AFTERWORD

Just when you think the wrestling business can't surprise you anymore, it finds a way. Right before this book went to press, the CM Punk saga took perhaps its most dramatic twist yet: at the conclusion of the annual Survivor Series, the Allstate Arena in Chicago (where else?) exploded as the opening riffs of 'Cult of Personality' unexpectedly bellowed through the building, disrupting the celebrations at the end of the men's War Games match. In the age of 24/7 wrestling news, this was the rarest of things: a story that stayed totally secret until the big reveal took place. CM Punk was back, after almost 10 years of a rift between himself and WWE that had often seemed irreparable.

It was both surreal and electrifying; a moment that immediately sparked the kind of debate that seems to follow Punk everywhere he goes. Seth Rollins seemed beside himself with rage at the unexpected appearance of a man he had publicly criticised so many times in the recent past, while Drew McIntyre stormed out of the auditorium in a hurry before the music even hit - were either of these planned story-line developments, or was Punk's notoriously disruptive

AFTERWORD

influence already being felt in a locker room that had apparently been remarkably harmonious in recent times? This blurring of the line between fact and fiction was exactly what Punk brings to the party - and exactly why he has long been among the most popular topics of conversation for wrestling fans around the world. This was - for now at least - an undisputed moment of triumph for WWE, and a moment for AEW fans to feel more trepidatious than ever about the future.

Every bit as intriguing as the return itself was the decision-making process behind it. Traditionally, Vince McMahon had been the architect of such major moves in WWE. However, in this instance, it was Nick Khan and Triple H who orchestrated Punk's return, confirming a significant shift in WWE's internal power structure that had been reported for the past few months. It had already been said that McMahon had been sidelined by Ari Emanuel in the weeks since the WWE-Endeavor merger was completed in early September, but this seemed to be the plainest evidence yet that those reports were accurate - the predictions of such a move that happened around WrestleMania week no longer seemed far-fetched to even the most sceptical of onlookers. The times really are changing.

The future, as always in professional wrestling, is rife with possibilities. CM Punk might be back in WWE, but AEW is not defeated - far from it. The war between the two sides rages on, and if the past 18 months have taught us anything, it's that we can never predict what will happen next. But then, that's the beauty of it all, isn't it? The story of professional wrestling, with its heroes, villains, and endless surprises, marches on, and we, the fans, are here for every captivating moment of it.

ABOUT THE AUTHORS

ABOUT WRESTLETALK

WrestleTalk is the world's biggest wrestling media brand, with over 1 million YouTube subscribers and around 8 million monthly video views across its main and sister channels. The WrestleTalk.com website is now the most viewed news site in the industry, generating around one hundred million page views annually. On top of this, the brand has expanded into various other areas, including the bi-monthly WrestleTalk Magazine (from which the articles in this book are taken), live events, and online merchandise store WrestleShop.com. Collectively these elements provide wrestling fans across the globe with all the news, entertainment and insight they need to get their full fix of the professional wrestling world.

ABOUT THE AUTHORS

Oli Davis first took over as the lead producer of WrestleTalk's YouTube channel at the start of 2016, having previously worked in production and live broadcast transmission for Channel 4, Bauer Media, ESPN, BT Sport and NBCU. As well as being a hugely popular on-air personality, he has overseen the brand's growth into multiple new areas such as podcasts, live events, broadcast television shows, live-streaming, print media, merchandise and WrestleTalk.com, which is now among the biggest wrestling news websites on the planet.

A lifelong wrestling fan, Dave Bradshaw has spent over 15 years as a play-by-play commentator and become one of the most recognisable voices in independent wrestling worldwide. He is also an NCTJ-trained journalist who regularly writes features for WrestleTalk Magazine and is currently preparing to author his first book. He has previously reported news for national and local media and also has experience working in the UK Parliament and in the higher education sector. Now working full time for WrestleTalk, he divides his time between writing content, developing new projects and coordinating the creative output across our channels.

John Ellul is a freelance journalist, media and communications professional, and former local newspaper reporter, based in Berkshire, UK. In addition to being a lifelong wrestling fan, he has been a regular contributor to WrestleTalk Magazine and website since 2020, writing features and columns on topics ranging from the death of WCW, to trouble at the top in WWE. In 2023 he self-published his first book, Flowers for Adrian: The Life and Death of Adrian Adonis, a biography on the life and legacy of the colourful former AWA and WWF tag-team champion.

H.G. McLaren is a writer and wrestling historian with over three decades of following the industry. He has written on topics covering the entire spectrum of subjects relating to professional wrestling, encompassing everything from the commercial side of the business to the unique personalities that have shaped the artform. As well as taking a major interest in the major US companies, he also closely follows developments in Japan, Mexico and Europe, as well as the North American independent scene.

Dee Adams is a passionate writer with a deep-rooted love for professional wrestling. A lifelong wrestling enthusiast, Dee's fervour for the sport is evident in her contributions to WrestleTalk Magazine, where she delves into the intricate world of wrestling, offering insights, reviews, and analyses. Beyond her wrestling commentary, Dee is an accomplished author, having already published two books with several more on the way.

THE MOST CRITICALLY ACCLAIMED
MAGAZINE IN WRESTLING
WRESTLETALK
MAGAZINE
"YOU'RE FIRED!"
THE SUMMER OF PUNK
WHO IS THE GREATEST OF ALL
MANIA TRIUMPHS
RE-ENTER THE DRAGON
WWE STRIKES BACK!
REVOLUTION
AVAILABLE NOW
WWW.WRESTLESHOP.COM

ALSO AVAILABLE ON
amazon kindle

RIPPING THE MASK OFF CRIME, POLITICS AND INTRIGUE BEYOND THE RING

WRESTLETALK

WRESTLING UNMASKED

RIPPING THE MASK OFF THE CRIME, POLITICS AND INTRIGUE BEYOND THE RING

GET YOUR COPY TODAY
E-BOOK JUST £6.99
PRINT EDITION £14.99

ORDER NOW
WWW.WRESTLESHOP.COM

Printed in Great Britain
by Amazon